AMERICAN
FOLKTALES * MYTHS * LEGENDS

AMERICAN
FOLKTALES * MYTHS * LEGENDS

Edited by LESLIE CONRON

Madison Park Press
New York

Developed by Arena Books Associates, LLC
www.arenabks.com

This edition first published by Madison Park Press by arrangement with
Arena Books Associates, LLC

ISBN: 978-1-61523-325-0

Cover Photograph © David Muench, David Muench Photography, Inc.

Sources:
Charles M. Skinner. *American Myths & Legends.* 2 vols. J. B. Lippincott Company, 1903.
From Vol. 1: "The Good Bird Spirit," "The Drinking of Sweet Water," "The Rescue of Molly
Finney," "A Travelled Narrative," "The Long Sleep," "The Gander's Message," "The
Golden Tooth," "How the Black Horse was Beaten," "Tom Dunn's Dance on Rag Rock,"
"How Bill Stout Settled a Mortgage," "A Gift from St. Nicholas." From Vol. 2: "The Climber
of the Teton," "The Enchanted Horse," "The Spectre Bride," "Indian Mermaids and Fairies."
Bertha H. Smith. *Yosemite Legends.* San Francisco: Paul Elder and Company, 1904
Sketches and Eccentricities of Col. David Crockett. New York: J & J. Harper, 1835.
Mark Twain. *Mark Twain's Sketches, New and Old,* 1875.
Mark Twain. *The Adventures of Tom Sawyer.* The American Publishing Company, 1876.
Joel Chandler Harris. *Uncle Remus and His Friends.* Houghton Mifflin and Company, 1892.
Glen Rounds. *Ol' Paul, the Mighty Logger.* New York: Holiday House, Inc. Copyright 1936,
by Holiday House, Inc.
Washington Irving. *Rip Van Winkle,* 1819.
Henry Wadsworth Longfellow. *The Song of Hiawatha,* 1855.
Clement C. Moore. *The Night Before Christmas,* 1823.
James MacGillivray. "The Round River Drive," *Detroit News,* July 24, 1910.
EdWard O'Reilly. "The Saga of Pecos Bill," *Century Magazine,* October 1923.
R. D. Haley. "Johnny Appleseed: A Pioneer Hero," *Harper's New Monthly Magazine,*
November 1871 (Vol. XLII, No. CLVIII).
Folksongs: "John Henry," "The Old Chisolm Trail," "The Cowboy Lament," "Git Along Little
Dogies" as appeared in John A. Lomax, "Some Types of American Folk-Song," *Journal of
American Folklore* 28, no. 107 (January-March 1915).

CONTENTS

INTRODUCTION

We are all fascinated by the magic of folktales, fairy tales, myths, and legends, and we love a good story. Often, but not always, handed down orally, these folkstories present traditional beliefs, history, and cultural perceptions modified and embellished in the telling. Tales told outdoors around a campfire cast a certain mystery. They offer a poetry, a music of their own. The tales, meant to be told or recited narratives, give fresh meaning to terms like magic and enchantment, as well as to our understanding of our own lives. Told aloud, often to groups of listeners, by many storytellers with individual variations in the telling, the tales are as individual as the tellers themselves. Storytellers embellish with decorative details to "lift" the stories, add a little spice. The spine of the story is present but the details may differ. Not all of the tales we have included have sprung from such an

oral tradition. Some were created by journalists and newspapermen, by literary writers, and at least one —Paul Bunyan—is thought to originate from a lumber company's advertising brochure. But the tales all flourished by being retold.

The romantic stories of the old West thrive in cowboy ballads. We think of loggers, miners, railroad workers, cowboys, pioneers, frontiersman of the old West gathered around a campfire at the end of a long, physically grueling day, filling the air with tales of crafty or heroic individuals. A cowboy might add a verse to a known ballad, one like "The Old Chisholm Trail." He might practice the verse as he rode the range alone on his horse during the day, and bring the rehearsed addition to the campfire in the evening. If approved by those assembled, the verse would be added to the song. And *there* is the wandering storyteller.

American folklore is like a large quilt with elements from many cultures, all brought together in one collective piece. The individual tales are very human: they reveal a way of thinking, a way of life, and a sense of place that is decidedly American, with all the accumulated differences. We have included a broad range of tales, myths, and legends that take us on a journey of America's past. We laugh, we cry, and we nod in agreement with them. We are moved by them. The stories range from a Native American legend of place names, like Yosemite; to the merry elf Logoodrie, the Puck of Native

American sprites; to Hiawatha, son of the West wind and grandson of the Moon; to an enchanted horse with magical powers; to a tale of Indian mermaids and fairies; to Davy Crockett's wonderfully silly *Grinning the Bark off the Tree.* Literary works like *Rip Van Winkle, The Adventures of Tom Sawyer,* and *Brer Rabbit* present folk characters that have become part of our everyday language. We have also included stories of memorable, larger-than-life folk heroes, like Pecos Bill and his bouncing bride Slue-Foot Sue, Paul Bunyan and Babe the Blue Ox, Johnny Appleseed, and John Henry. Born in the American imagination, these characters represent strength, vitality, competence, courage, and all the grand virtues of the American pioneers who conquered the wilderness with all its obstacles.

We have gathered the tales from several sources, and have retained the spellings and punctuations from those sources. Read one, or two. Better yet, read a tale as it was meant to be read—aloud. And then tell that tale to a friend or a group of friends, adjusting the story itself or the way you tell it to your audience. Listen to the cadence and rhythm of the language. Let it carry you along. You are a storyteller.

Most of the tales are entertaining, many are exhilarating, some are heart-breakingly poignant, and others are laugh-out-loud funny. But they are all informative: they remind us who we are.

THE CLIMBER OF THE TETON
CHARLES M. SKINNER

In 1898 the Grand Teton moun-
tain in Wyoming was scaled for the first time by a company of
white men. It's height, 13,800 feet, is less than that of a dozen
mountains in the Rockies that have been ascended safely, but
there are few if any more savage in difficulties and terrible in
contour. Tall as are the precipices of the Matterhorn, they lack
by thousands of feet the sublimity of the Teton's western rise,
which for nearly two miles is vertical. The Indians have long
held this peak in reverence. That is a safe emotion. The trav-
eller who can persuade himself into a great fear of such a peak
will never climb it, and if he never climbs it he avoids work.
Before the white race had ever dazzled its eyes with the snows
of this Alp a tribe of Indians camped in Jackson's Hole, almost
in its shadow. That little valley contained game, which was to

be had without much trouble; but the braves, used to exhilarating combat, grew bored with the lack of enemies to fight.
As an outlet for their energy and a test of courage, it was pro-
posed that all the younger men should climb the Grand Teton.
They made the attempt, but none of them reached the top.
Miniwepta, belle of their company, teased them for their fail-
ure and said that she would show the clumsy fellows how to
reach the summit. Early in the morning she slipped out of
camp on a pony. Her relatives followed, in fear of some rash
and tomboyish exploit on her part, until they lost the trail, at
nightfall. As it became dark they saw a fire burning on the
mountain-side. Next night another fire appeared, higher
among the crags. On the third night a red spark glowed and
glimmered away up on the precipice, a few hundred feet
below the summit. On the fourth night no fire was seen.
Miniwepta's people rode homeward in silence.

THE GOOD BIRD SPIRIT
CHARLES M. SKINNER

In the country called Kaya-
derossera, in and about Saratoga, New York are many battle-
grounds where tribes of old contended for supremacy. The
fields about the healing waters that in our time are every summer resorted to by thousands were held by the Mohawks and
they were under the protection of many manitous, none of
whom were more kind than the good bird spirit. Though usually wearing the form of a white dove, the Manitou would take
the shape of an enemy and suffer itself to be killed, when it
would rise again in its bird shape, guide the straggler back to
his camp, and even restore the dead to life. A hunter who had
missed the trail and was wandering through the forest saw a

gray owl on a branch that overhung him, and heard its hoot. It is a common belief that in the rare accident of an Indian's losing his way some evil influence is working against him, that he is doomed to wander in a circle until he is exhausted, the circles growing smaller as he nears the place of the demon. To his excited fancy this bird was a fiend and was mocking his distress. He slipped an arrow on his bow-string and shot the creature through. It fell fluttering to the earth, where he would have dispatched it with his axe had not a dove sprung from the body and soared above his head. The brooding clouds broke away, the hunter's moon struck its light through the branches, making the new snow to sparkle, and the despair in the man's heart gave way to thankfulness, for he realized that he had been rescued by the spirit of the wood; and, following his guide in its slow flight, he presently emerged on the shore of Saratoga Lake at the point where he had left his canoe three days before.

Among most Indian tribes physical courage is the highest virtue, and young men must endure injuries and disfigurements to prove their bravery. If they fail, they suffer the contempt of men and women alike. In the old days girls as well as young men had to prove their strength and ability to suffer uncomplainingly, that it might be known if they were fit to become wives of fighters and mothers of heroes. Saratoga Lake was a frequent scene of these tests, for it was customary

to force the maidens, in their thirteenth year, to swim from the mouth of Kayaderosseras River to the Hill of Storms, now called Snake Hill. The Mohawks were never a stronger people than when they gathered at this water to see the daughter of their chief, his only child, cross it, or drown in the attempt as one not worthy of being a princess. In the moon of green corn the day had been set. The father led the girl to the canoe that was to take her to the other shore and bade her be of good heart. She paddled across, disembarked, tossed off her clothing, and plunged boldly, lightly, into the lake, the old man watching for her, anxiously. It was a long way, the wind had veered so as to baffle the swimmer, and the waves were rising. Her progress grew slower and slower. She turned on her back and floated for a little to regain breath and strength, thus drifting away again. It was plain that she was exhausted. Feebly moving forward once more, she began her death-song. Her father's face was a picture of woe. Suddenly, a shout of astonishment from the people; a great eagle, darting from the clouds, struck his talons into her hair and tried to lift her. She caught him by the legs, then both disappeared beneath the surface. A moan came from the company, then a cry of gladness. Out of the dark water a dove had flown, and, rising to her feet in a shallow, the girl had reappeared. While wading to the shore, where a score of arms were held toward her, the dove circled, then alighted on her head and remained there

until she had reached firm ground. The sudden rack of pain and joy was too much for her father. With a look of gratitude at the sky, into which the dove was now ascending, he ceased to breathe. So the girl was queen of the Mohawks, and for long after it was the daughter, not the son, who succeeded to chief. The dove became the tribal token.

Once, in the moon of roses, five hundred Mohawks marching northward met a party of Algonquins coming from Canada. The Mohawks, who were of that great family, the Iroquois, "the Romans of the West," were on ill terms with their neighbors of the cold lands, calling them Adirondacks (tree-eaters), because when game was scarce in the biting winters they stripped the trees of buds, gum, and inner bark, for food. It was near the site of Ballston that they met this time, and a fight began at once. While it raged an eagle, sniffing blood and hoping to find prey among creatures so wasteful of life, hovered above the field, now trampled and sodden with gore, yet only an hour ago a flowery meadow, sweet smelling and peaceful in the sun. Weary with its flight it settled on a pine as the day was ending, and still watched the exhausted savages as they struck and parried, and shot, and slew, and scalped. Its screams had given heart to both armies, but now they began to believe that it was an evil creature who had lured them to this slaughter. As by common consent the bow-man on both sides shot a flight of arrows at the bird; so many

that arrows followed one another through the same wound.
Directly that it had fallen into the deep grass a shining dove
arose from the spot and perched on the branch from which the
eagle had fallen: the good bird spirit; the dove of peace.
Arrows that were being fitted to the bows dropped to the
ground. The men seemed as if waking from an ugly dream.
The chiefs moved toward each other, their heads hung in sorrow as they looked on the corpses of their brothers slain in
useless rage for a feud of forgotten origin. There was a long
talk. Then both sides gathered around a fire and smoked the
pipe of friendship. Because of the killing on that day the
stream whose waters ran red is still the Mourning Kill.

THE ENCHANTED HORSE
CHARLES M. SKINNER

Among the Pawnee Indians living on the North Platte of the Dakota plains long ago were a woman and her grandson who were so poor they embarrassed the tribe. Their clothing, shoes, weapons all were rescued from what other members of the tribe had discarded. Their teepee leaked through its many patches, their robes had lost half their fur, and they lived on scraps of meat rejected by the others.

Somehow, the boy comforted his grandmother with the assurance that when he became a man he would kill buffalo like the rest, and they would have a painted lodge and clothing adorned with quills and beads. When the tribe was preparing for a seasonal move to better hunting grounds, the young boy

found browsing among the refuse of the village a sorry old horse, half-blind, lame, and sway-backed. The horse certainly did not look like much, but there was something, just something, about him that inspired the young boy to bring him to his grandmother. "He's not pretty, but he can carry our little pack." The boy was gentle with the horse, taking care not to push him too hard. And the horse was grateful. The new camp had been set up for much of the day by the time the young boy, his grandmother, and the rickety old horse carrying their few, tattered possessions arrived at the new village.

The chief gathered the men about him and said that a large herd of buffalo had been spotted about four miles away, and among them was a spotted calf. A spotted buffalo robe is rare and considered a good omen, conferring success and fortune on its owner. The chief offered his daughter in marriage to the brave who returned from the chase with the magic skin. To give all an equal chance, the hunters would leave the camp together, as in a race. The boy took his handful of crooked arrows, his cracked bow, and stood and looked at his poor excuse for a horse thinking that the poor old thing would just collapse if he ever tried to run to keep up with the other hunters. But the horse looked him straight in the eye. "Drive me to the river and plaster me with mud," he said. The boy almost fainted hearing the human voice coming from the horse. But, collecting his wits, he did just as the horse instruct-

ed. "Now," continued the horse, "climb on my back and when the word is given let me have free reign, let me fly!"

As he took his place with the bucks, they roared with laughter at the sight of the boy on his ungainly sad-sack-presumption-of-a-horse caked with mud. The boy turned away with his heart sinking. How he hated being poor. But he was determined to be the first to find the spotted calf and bring its skin back to the chief and thereby bring honor and comfort to his grandmother and himself. He would beat those hunters in the race and he would marry the chief's daughter.

All were ready, "Go," cried the chief, and the line of young hunters rushed forward with wild whoops, ignoring the young boy on his ridiculous, mud-covered horse. The confident leaders of the pack sat up proudly on their steeds, as if they grew straight from their horses' backs. A sudden sharp cry of astonishment caused all eyes to look left, as the old dun horse and his young rider passed them with such ease that he seemed not to be running at all, but flying across the earth like a hawk rising on updraft of wind with outspread wings. Straight toward the spotted calf raced the boy, before the others had even seen it in the pack of shaggy backs, and with a single shot he killed it. While he skinned the animal his horse pranced in circles around him like a colt. His age, lameness, and blindness had disappeared.

As the boy tramped back to the village with the meat

and the spotted hide bound upon his horse's back the people stared with wonder. A brave offered twelve ponies for the skin, but the lad shook his head and went on to the mean little lodge he shared with his grandmother. She cleaned and dressed the trophy and prepared a generous meal of the meat. That evening the animal spoke again as the young brave was grooming him: "The Sioux are coming. When they attack tomorrow mount me, gallop straight against the chief, kill him, and ride back. Do this four times, killing a Sioux at each charge. Do not go a fifth time, for you may lose me or be killed yourself." That night the boy mended his weapons and painted his face; and in the morning things happened as the horse predicted. The boy killed four Sioux and returned to the camp with their axes. He had proved his bravery, and some of the sturdiest fighters of the clan patted his head and spoke kindly to him. The excitement of the battle had seized him and he could not resist another attack. But the fifth strike brought disaster. His brave horse fell under a Sioux arrow, and the enemy cut him into pieces so that he might never bear another Pawnee on his back.

Though the boy had fled in safety to his own lines, he was despondent over the loss of his horse. After nightfall when the Sioux had retreated, he collected the bones of his horse, brought them back to camp, and pieced them together. Then, with the spotted robe drawn over his head, he mourned

his steed. A great wind arose, bringing a rain that washed away the blood and freshened the grass. To the boy the rain was like tears, and the pain he felt was just punishment for disobeying this wise and faithful animal. After he had mourned for several hours he looked up to see that the severed limbs and head had arranged themselves in a life-like attitude. Then the tail flicked, the animal arose, walked to the boy and said, "The Great Spirit is kind. He has let me come back to life. You have had your lesson. Hereafter, remember to trust me."

In the morning the horse was as sound as ever, and during the rest of his long life he was honored by the people, while the boy established his grandmother in comfort, married the chief's daughter, and in the end became chief himself.

Yosemite:
Large Grizzly Bear
Bertha H. Smith

When the world was made, the Great Spirit tore out the heart of Kay-o-pha, the Sky Mountains, and left the gash unhealed. He sent the Coyote to people the valley with a strong and hardy race of men who called their home Ah-wah-nee, and themselves, the Ah-wah-nee-chees.

The Ah-wah-nee-chees lived the simple, savage life, which knows no law but to hunt and kill and eat. By day the trackless forest rang with the clamor of the chase. By the flaring light of their fires the hunters gorged themselves upon the fresh-killed meat, feasting far into the night. They made war

upon the tribes that lived beyond the walls of Ah-wah-nee and never knew defeat, for none dared follow them to their rock-ribbed fastness. They were feared by all save the outcasts of other tribes, whose lawless deeds won for them a place among the Ah-wah-nee-chees. Thus the children of Ah-wah-nee increased in number and strength. As time went by, the Ah-wah-ne-chees, in their pride of power, forgot the Great Spirit who had given them their stronghold and made them feared of all their race, And the Great Spirit, turning upon them in his wrath, loosed his evil forces in their midst, scourging them with a black sickness that swept all before it as a hot wind blights the grain at harvest time.

The air of the valley was a poison breath, in which the death shade hovered darkly. Before the Evil Spirit medicine men were powerless. Their mystic spells and incantations were a weird mockery, performed among the dying and the dead; and when at last the Evil One passed onward in his cursed flight, the once proud and powerful band of Ah-wah-nee-chees was like a straggling pack of gaunt gray wolves. Their eyes gleamed dully in their shrunken faces, and the skin hung in loose folds on their wasted bodies.

Those who were able fled from the valley, which was now a haunted place, eerie with flitting shadows of funeral fires and ghostly echoes of the funeral wail. They scattered among the tribes beyond the mountains, and Ah-wah-nee was deserted.

A vast stillness settled upon the valley, broken only by

the songs of birds and the roar of Cho-look when Spring sent the mountain torrents crashing over his head. The mountain lion and the grizzly roamed at will among the rocks and tangled chinquapin, fearless of arrows; the doe led her young by an open path to the river, where trout flashed their colors boldly in the sun. In the autumn the choke-cherries and manzanita berries dried upon their stems, and ripened acorns rotted to dust upon the ground after the squirrels had gathered their winter store. The homeless Ah-wah-nee-chees circled wide in passing the valley.

Over beyond To-co-yah, the North Dome, among the Mo-nos and Pai-u-tes, a few of the ill-fated Ah-wah-nee-chees had found refuge. Among them was the chief of the tribe, who after a time took a Mo-no maiden for his bride. By this Mo-no woman he had a son, and they gave him the name of Ten-ie-ya. Before another round of seasons, the spirit of the Ah-wah-nee-chee chieftain had wandered on to the Land of the Sun, the home of happy souls.

Ten-ie-ya grew up among his mother's people, but the fire of a warrior chief was in his blood and he liked not to live where the word of another was law. The fire in his blood was kept aflame by the words of an old man, the patriarch of his father's tribe, who urged him to return to Ah-wah-nee, the home of his ancestors, and gather about him the people whose chief he was by right of birth.

So, Ten-ie-ya went back across the mountains by a

trail abandoned long ago, and from the camps of other tribes came those in whose veins was any trace of Ah-wah-nee-chee blood; and, as before, the number was increased by lawless braves of weaker bands who liked a greater freedom for their lawlessness. Again, under the favor of the Great Spirit, the Ah-wah-nee-chees flourished and by their fierce strength and daring became to other tribes as the mountain lion to the wolf and the coyote and the mountain sheep.

And it chanced that one day while Ten-ie-ya and his warriors were camped near Le-ham-i-te, the Canon of the Arrow-wood, a young brave went out in the early morning to the lake of Ke-koo-too-yem, the Sleeping Water, to spear fish. His lithe, strong limbs took no heed of the rocky talus in his path, and he leaped from boulder to boulder, following the wall that rose sheer above him and cut the blue sky overhead.

As he reached the base of Scho-ko-ni, the cliff that arches like the shade of an Indian cradle basket, he came suddenly upon a monster grizzly that had just crept forth from his winter cave. The grizzly knows no man for his friend; least of all, the man who surprises him at the first meal after his long sleep. The rivals of Ah-wah-nee were face to face.

The Ah-wah-nee-chee had no weapon save his fish spear, useless as a reed; yet he had the fearlessness of youth and the courage of a race to whom valorous deeds are more than strings of wampum, piles of pelt or many cattle. He faced

the grizzly boldly as the clumsy hulk rose to its full height, at bay and keen for attack. With instinctive love of conflict roused, the young chief seized a broken limb that lay at his feet, and gave the grizzly blow for blow.

The claws of the maddened brute raked his flesh. The blood ran warm over his glistening skin and matted the bristled yellow fur of the grizzly.

The Ah-wah-nee-chee fought bravely. While there was blood in his body, he could fight; when the blood was gone, he could die; but with the traditions of his ancestors firing his brain, he could not flee.

Furious with pain, blinded by the blows from the young chief's club and by the blood from the young chief's torn flesh, the grizzly struggled savagely. He, too, was driven by the law of his breed, the universal law of the forest, the law of Indian and grizzly alike,—which is to kill.

Such a battle could not last. With a low growl the crippled grizzly brought himself together and struck with the full force of his powerful arm. The blow fell short.

Urging his waning strength to one last effort, the Ah-wah-nee-chee raised his club high above his head and brought it down with a heavy, well-aimed stroke that crushed the grizzly's skull and sent him rolling among the boulders, dead.

That night as the Ah-wah-nee-chees feasted themselves on bear meat, the story of the young chief's bravery was

told, and told again; and from that hour he was known as Yo-sem-i-te, the Large Grizzly Bear.

In time the name Yo-sem-i-te was given to all the tribe of Ah-wah-nee-chees, who for fearlessness and lawlessness were rivaled only by the grizzly with whom they shared the mountain fastness. And when long afterward the white man came and took Ah-wah-nee for his own, he gave it the name by which Ten-ie-ya's band was known; and Cho-look, the high fall that makes the earth tremble with its mighty roar, he also called by the name of the large Grizzly Bear, Yo-sem-i-te.

TU-TOCK-AH-NU-LAH
AND TIS-SA-ACK
BERTHA H. SMITH

Since the world was young Tu-tock-ah-nu-lah, the Rock Chief, had guarded Ah-wah-nee, the home of the children of the sun. For his watch-tower he chose a storm-tried rock on the northern wall of the valley, and from this far height defied all the powers of evil.

In the spring he besought the Great Spirit to send rain that the wild corn might hang heavy with tasseling grain, the berries cluster thick on the branches of the manzanita, and the fish abound in the waters of the river. In the summer he fattened the bear and deer, and in the autumn he wandered through the mountains driving them from their haunts that the

hunter might not return empty-handed from the chase. The smoke of his pipe spread like a soft haze through the air, sheltering the women from the sun when they went forth to gather acorns and wood for winter.

His form was like a spear, straight and strong; and he reared his head high above the clouds. In his arm was the strength of an untamed grizzly; and his voice was like the sound of Cho-look, the great fall that thunders down from the north, starting deep echoes from crag and gorge. When the sunlight danced upon the water, the Ah-wah-nee-chees were happy, for they knew that Tu-tock-ah-nu-lah smiled; when the sky was overcast, they trembled, fearful of his frown; when his sighs swept mournfully through the pines, they, too, were sad. The children of Ah-wah-nee loved the mighty Rock Chief who dwelt above them in his lonely lodge.

One morning, as his midnight watch drew to a close and the first pale glint of day shone on his forehead, he heard a soft voice whisper, "Tu-tock-ah-nu-lah!"

His eyes burned with the passion fire as a fair vision rose before him, yonder on the granite dome of the southern wall. It was the form of a maiden, not of the dark tribe he loved and guarded, but fairer than any he had seen or known in dreams. Her face had the rosy flush of dawn, her eyes took their color from the morning sky, and her hair was like strands of golden sunlight. Her voice was low as a dove

call when she whispered Tu-tock-ah-nu-lah's name.

For a moment she lingered, smiling; but even as the Rock Chief leaped from his tower in answer to her call, she glided across the rounded dome and faded from his sight, leaving her throne shrouded in a snowy cloud. Piqued by the mystery of her flight, Tu-tock-ah-nu-lah flowed the sound of her rushing garments, wandering all day over the mountains; but the pine trees wove a blue mist about her, hiding her from his eyes. Not until he returned to his citadel at night did he see her face again. Then for an instant she appeared upon her throne, her pale brow tinged with the rose glow of the sun; and he knew that she was Tis-sa-ack, the Godess of the Valley, who shared with him the loving care of the Ah-wah-nee-chees.

Every morning now at dawn Tu-tock-ah-nu-lah left his tower and sped across the valley to meet the lovely goddess of his heart's desire. Through the day he hovered near her, gazing upon the fair form, always half hidden by billowing cloud, trying to read an answering love in her wide blue eyes. But never again did he hear the voice that came to him across the stillness of that one gray dawn.

Tu-tock-ah-nu-lah's passion grew day by day, as summer ripens the fruit of springtime budding; but Tis-sa-ack had no joy in his love. Her heart was heavy with a great sorrow, for she saw that the Rock Chief was blind to the needs of his people, that he had forsaken those who looked to him for life.

The sun burned his way through the sky, and no rains fell to cool the aching earth. Tu-tock-ah-nu-lah paid no heed to the withering leaves of the wild corn, the shrunken streams from which the fishermen turned with empty nets, the shriveling acorns that fell worthless to the ground. He neither knew nor cared that the hunter, after weary days in the mountains, came to his lodge at night with arrows unused, to meet the anxious glance of starving women and hear the wailing cry of hungry children.

The Ah-wah-nee-chees called upon the Rock Chief in vain. He did not hear their cries; he thought only of his love. The harvest moon looked down into the valley and saw the dark form of Famine skulking there. Then it was that Tis-sa-ack's love was swept away by an overwhelming pity; and as she lay upon her couch she cried to the Great Spirit to send the rain-clouds that bear life to all things of the earth.

And even as she prayed, there came an answer to her prayer. With a voice of thunder the Great Spirit gave commands to the spirits of the air. With a barbed shaft of lightening he rent the granite dome where Tis-sa-ack prayed; and from the cleft rock came a rush of water that filled the dry basin of Wai-ack, the Mirror Lake, and sent a wandering stream through the thirsty fields.

Now the withered corn-stalks raised their drooping heads, flowers nodded among the waving grasses and offered

their lips to the wild bees, and the acorns swelled with sap that crept upward from reviving roots. The women went joyously into the fields to gather the harvest, and the men no longer returned with empty pouches from the forest or fished by the riverside in vain.

The chief of the Ah-wah-nee-chees ordered a great feast, and all the faces were turned in gratitude to the dome where Tis-sa-ack dwelt. But Tis-sa-ack was gone. She had sacrificed her love, her life, for the children of Ah-wah-nee. Through her they had suffered; through her their sufferings had ceased; and that all might hold her memory dear she left them the lake, the river and a fragment of her throne. Upon the bosom of Ke-koo-too-yem, the Sleeping Water, her spirit rests, wandering sometimes of a summer evening to the Half Dome, there to linger for a moment as the sun slips over the western wall of the valley.

As she flew away a soft down from her wings fell upon the earth; and where it fell, along the edge of the river and over the meadows stretching toward Tu-tock-ah-nu-lah's watch-tower, one can now find tiny white violets, whose fragrance is the secret of a loving spirit, a breath of happiness to all who gather them.

When Tu-tock-ah-lu-nah found that Tis-sa-ack was gone, a great sadness came upon him. Day and night his sighs swept through the pine trees. He puffed gloomily at his pipe

until his tower was hidden in a cloud of smoke. At last, thinking to follow and find his lost love, he went away; and lest he be forgotten, he carved with his hunting knife the outlines of his face upon the wall of his fortress, which the white man has named El Capitan.

As he turned sadly from his lodge, Tu-tock-ah-nu-lah perceived that the air was filled with a rare and subtle perfume, blowing from a stretch of meadow fringed with tamarack. Thinking it the breath of Tis-sa-ack, he followed on and on, forgetful of the arts of E-ee-ke-no, who dwells among the water-lilies in the lake which the Three Brothers hold in the hollow of their hands.

E-ee-ke-no had long loved the Rock Chief, but Tu-tock-ah-nu-lah scorned her unsought love, which turned through jealousy to bitter hate. Now as she saw him go away in search of Tis-sa-ack, she threw around him the mystic fragrance of the water-lily, which, gentle as a caress, is deadly to all who win the hatred of E-ee-ke-no.

On and on across the meadow fringed with tamarack, among the wild flowers and the waving grasses, Tu-tock-ah-nu-lah wandered, following blindly the transformed spirit of E-ee-ke-no until he disappeared forever in the depths of the lake.

THE DRINKING
OF SWEET WATER
CHARLES M. SKINNER

Logoochie, the Puck of Indian sprites that flitted about the swamps and woods of Georgia, was not with the wood divinities when they met on the Flower Island of Okefinokee to discuss the strange race that had landed on the shores. For, though Logoochie was a merry elf, whose tricks and whims amused the other spirits, he so loved the Southland woods and waters that he would not listen to any talk of leaving them. He hid in a hollow tree and gave himself to bitter thought. Saltilla, three-eyed messenger of the gods, sought for hours through his play-grounds, but did not

find him. Like the moths and beetles that imitate the leaves and bark they rest against, he was not easy to see, when he chose to remain quiet; for his face was brown and wrinkled, his cheeks were puckered like pine-knots; his back was rough as a pine-cone; his little red eyes snapped and twinkled when they were open, but when shut you did not see the wrinkles where they had disappeared; his nose was flat, his mouth was wide, he was short, bow-legged, and his knobbed hands ended in claws, like a panther's. Yet, with all his ugliness of look he was gentle, and the hunters hated him only because he turned aside their spears and arrows when they went to slay the deer.

The spirits resolved to leave their home in the woods and follow the Creek Nation to the West, where other tribes were assembling; but Logoochie stayed. Sometimes at night-fall he could be seen scampering among the pines and savan-nas, startling the red laggers, and even more the white pio-neers who were setting up strange lodges on the Sweet Water—the village they called St. Mary's. Trees began to fall under the white man's axe. Logoochie crept to their houses in the night, and bent and gnawed their tools, till he saw that with a magic of their own they made them straight again.

Then that which so often happens among men befell Logoochie. From fear and hate he grew to tolerance. He could not leave his country vexed and blighted as it was. And he

even found a new pleasure in frightening these pale faces till they grew yet paler. He would drop into their paths, almost under their feet, as they returned from the hunt, and startle them with a squeal or a hiss. He would bound upon their shoulders from an overhanging bough; and before they had caught breath again he was lost in the undergrowth, and they heard his shrill, defiant laugh going into the distance. He would make threatening faces at them from the copse as they went to their day's work, and at night he would prowl along the edges of their town and sound the call of fierce animals.

But they were not such a bad people, after all, these men with the sick faces. They fought less than the red men; they never scalped and tortured; sometimes it seemed as if they were being good, The wood sprite shuddered when he heard the crash and groaning of the trees under the saws and axes, but he spread his nostrils and enjoyed the flavor when the cutters smoked in their camps at evening,—for they smoked more furiously than the Indians, and tobacco was Logoochie's special incense.

A girl of the settlement, wandering by the Sweet Water, came upon the imp, who was goggling fearfully, gasping, grunting, and hugging his foot. The poor creature was suffering, and although it cost an effort to overcome her repugnance, she went to his help. He had alighted on a thorn, as he leaped from a tree. She withdrew the thorn and bound healing

leaves upon the wound—a service that he acknowledged in the most frightening grins and gibbering. Indeed, he went through such antics in his joy that the maid was like to faint from dread. Yet, he had a voice that was almost music; it was a voice she had often heard in the pines, and had never understood, till now. He said: "The daughter of the white people is good. She shall never come to harm in the forest. The green people of the wood will watch her when she rambles by the water. If she sleeps, they will shadow her face and sing drowsy songs in the branches. They will drive away the snake if it comes near, and they will whisper comfort if she has sorrow. This, and more: If the white maid suffers from forgetfulness, she shall bring her lover back, through the spell I put upon this water."

The fright of the girl had passed, and a blush appeared. Her eyes fell under the gaze of the elf. He chuckled, as in delight at his own shrewdness, for he had guessed her secret. She loved an adventurous fellow of St. Mary's, who that very day told her he had resolved to be a sailor that he might see the wonders of the deep, and strange countries, and wrest treasure from the enemies of the king. She could not consent to this, even if the treasure were that of the king himself. Beyond all fame and riches she held himself.

Logoochie plucked red berries from a bush that overhung the water and cast them into the middle of the stream,

muttering strange words and waving his arms. The stream boiled, and a little whirlpool appeared. Then the berries were drawn down, and the surface was still again. "Make him drink of this," whispered the sprite, and with a bound he disappeared into the wood.

That night, when the moon was rising and balmy odors breathed from the forest, the lovers walked beside the branch of Sweet Water. It was to be their last walk together. Tears brimmed from the girl's eyes, and the young man was silent and thoughtful. When they reached the place where they had been used to rest during their rambles the girl dipped a gourd into the stream and gave it to her lover. He emptied it at a draught, refilled it, and gave it to her. She too drank from it. And he did not go to sea, and the girl was a happy bride soon after. Logoochie disappeared, but his spell still lives, and they who drink of the charmed flood will never leave the country of the Sweet Water.

THE SWAN OF LIGHT
CHARLES M. SKINNER

There was no island on Horn Pond, Massachusetts, in the long ago. When it was Lake Initou the red men worshiped so many lesser gods that they had no time to praise the one Master of Life. So it chanced that signs of anger were seen on the earth and in the heavens. Lake Initou, Mirror of the Spirit, was dark and troubled even in the calmest weather. Flashes of light and unaccountable sounds were seen and heard on Towanda and Mianomo. Then the game fled away, the fish grew scarce, the roots and berries suffered from a blight. As Chief Wakima lay in sleep on the lake shore he saw through his closed lids a growing light, and, opening his eyes, beheld a luminous boat advancing, self-driv-

en, across the water, bearing a tall and beautiful form that also shone in white. The chief sprang to his feet in amazement, but sank to his knees again in awe when the boat grounded on the beach and the messenger stood before him, looking down with a face of sorrow and rebuke.

The shining one said: "You pray to the air, to the lake, to the trees, that your people may not suffer from disease and hunger, from the heat of summer and the winter frosts.You do not appeal to the Spirit that rules all lesser ones and all the earth. Are your prayers to the manitous of the woods and waters answered? No; you have only sickness, famine, disappointment. Bid your medicine-men stop their follies, their shaking of rattles, their chants, their ceremonies, and address their words to Him who bends from the clouds to listen and is sorry to hear no voice of His children. When your people have prayed properly, gather them at the water-side, and if you have been true and good the Great Spirit will give a sign that He loves you."

Wakima raised his head to answer but found himself alone. The vision seemed like a dream. Yet in his heart he knew he had offended. He would obey the shining one. He told his prophets what had been told to him, and ere long the game returned to the hills, the fish to the waters, the fruits were sweet and plenty, and the young grew fast and strong. When the Moon of Flowers had come Wakima recalled the promise

of the messenger and gathered his people on the lake in their canoes to wait the sign. Gradually the boats, as of some will of their own, drifted into a circle, and in the middle of this ring, deep down, a light began to glow. It became brighter and brighter as it neared the surface, and presently arose in the air a gigantic swan, that shone with a glorious white light, as silver would shine in the sun. It spread its vast wings till they covered all the tribe as in token of blessing; then it settled on the water again and sank, the light paling as slowly as it had grown. When it had disappeared something dark rose silently from the lake, and in the morning an island stood there—the island that the red men called the Swan.

THE SPECTRE BRIDE
CHARLES M. SKINNER

Fighting Buffalo, a young hunter of the Osages, left camp on the Nickanansa to sell his furs in St. Louis and to buy there some ornaments worthy to be worn by Prairie Flower, the girl who had promised to marry him, on his return. This journey, eighty or ninety years ago, was a matter of toil and difficulty, so that he was absent for about three weeks, during which time he had no news of affairs at home. When he regained the Nickanansa and had neared the site of his village he quickened his pace, for there were no lodge peaks above the earth waves of the prairie, no wisps of smoke to promise the comfort of supper. Not greatly wondering at this, as he knew and shared the migratory habits of his people,

he looked about to see some picture-writing that should guide him to the new village of the tribe, and was pleasantly surprised on seeing at a distance the figure of a young woman, seated among the ashes and refuse of the vanished camp, and bent, as if weeping. The pleasure of this discovery was in the recognition of the girl. It was Prairie Flower. He ran forward eagerly, and would have embraced her, but she turned her head sadly, and would not look at him.

"I have jewels and ribbons for you, my bride," he said tossing off his pack.

She gave a little sob.

"Where are our people?" he asked.

"Gone. Gone to the Wagrushka."

"But you are here, alone."

"I was waiting for you."

"Then we will go to our people at once, and tomorrow we shall be married; and you will be the most beautiful of all the girls; yes, in all the flat country."

She still averted her face. "I will carry your pack," she said. Among Indians the burdens that are not borne by horses are usually carried by women, so this was quite the thing to do. Fighting Buffalo laughed a little as his sweetheart picked up the bundle, for it was filled with gifts that would make her happy. But why did she hide her face? And now that they had started on the march for the Wagrushka, why did she gather

her cloak about her in that fashion, and cover her head, like the head of a corpse that is ready for burial? "There's no accounting for women's tempers," thought the hunter. "She will be more kind tomorrow." Plodding on through the tall grass, she following silently in his footsteps, seldom speaking, and then but quietly, they came at sunset to the new camp of the Osages and saw the blue smoke curling pleasantly above the tepees. The girl stopped. "It is better that we should not enter the camp together. You know that is the custom only with married people. I will wait for a time beneath this tree."

Fighting Buffalo ran on ahead, aroused the village with a joyful shout, and called greetings to his relatives, while yet a quarter of a mile away. Tomorrow Prairie Flower would be his wife, and he was happy. As he went nearer he was chilled by a boding. The people were sad and silent. Even the children desisted from their play. "What ails you all?" he asked. "Has any one died since I left you?"

There was no answer. Then he addressed his sister: "Feather Cloud, go back and tell Prairie Flower to come to us." His sister recoiled. "Do not speak like that," she murmured, with a sidelong glance toward her parents, as if she feared they might have heard her brother's words.

"Tell me, what has come over every one? Why have you moved? Why will you not bring my bride to me?"

"Prairie Flower is dead, and is buried beneath that tree."

"This is poor fun, if you intend to joke. She came with me from the Nickanansa, and brought my pack as far as that tree. Faugh! I will go after her myself."

He walked hastily back in the twilight, his people following at a distance. His pack lay at the tree-foot, on a new grave. With a choking cry he pressed his hands upon his heart and fell on the mound, dead.

HIAWATHA'S CHILDHOOD
HENRY WADSWORTH LONGFELLOW

Downward through the evening twilight,
In the days that are forgotten,
In the unremembered ages,
From the full moon fell Nokomis,
Fell the beautiful Nokomis,
She a wife, but not a mother.
      She was sporting with her women
Swinging in a swing of grapevines,
When her rival, the rejected,
Full of jealousy and hatred,
Cut the leaf swing asunder,

From *The Song of Hiawatha*

Cut in twain the twisted grapevines,
And Nokomis fell affrighted
Downward through the evening twilight,
On the Muskoday, the meadow,
On the prairie full of blossoms.
"See! A star falls!" said the people;
"From the sky a star is falling!"
There among the ferns and mosses,
There among the prairie lilies,
On the Muskoday the meadow,
In the moonlight and the starlight,
Fair Nokomis bore a daughter.
And she called her name Wenonah,
As the first born of her daughters.
And the daughter of Nokomis
Grew up like the prairie lilies,
Grew a tall and slender maiden,
With the beauty of the moonlight,
With the beauty of the starlight.
    And Nokomis warned her often,
Saying oft, and oft repeating,
"O, beware of Mudjekeewis,
Of the West-Wind, Mudjekeewis,
Listen not to what he tells you;
Lie not down upon the meadow,

Stoop not down among the lilies,
Lest the West-Wind come and harm you!"
    But she heeded not the warning,
Heeded not those words of wisdom,
And the West-Wind came at evening,
Walking lightly o'er the prairie,
Whispering to the leaves and blossoms,
Bending low the flowers and grasses,
Found the beautiful Wenonah,
Lying there among the lilies,
Wooed her with his words of sweetness,
Wooed her with his soft caresses,
Till she bore a son in sorrow,
Bore a son of love and sorrow.

    Thus was born my Hiawatha,
Thus was born the child of wonder;
But the daughter of Nokomis,
Hiawatha's gentle mother,
In her anguish died deserted
By The West-Wind, false and faithless,
By the heartless Mudjekeewis.

    For her daughter, long and loudly
Wailed and wept the sad Nokomis;
"O that I were dead!" she murmured,
'O that I were dead, as thou art

No more work, and no more weeping,
Wahonowin! Wahonowin!"
    By the shores of Gitche Gumee.
By the shining Big-Sea-Water
Stood the wigwam of Nokomis.
Daughter of the Moon, Nokomis,
Dark behind it rose the forest,
Rose the black and gloomy pine-trees,
Rose the firs with cones upon them;
Bright before it beat the water,
Beat the clear and sunny water,
Beat the shining Big-Sea-Water.
    There the wrinkled, old Nokomis
Nursed the little Hiawatha,
Rocked him in his linen cradle,
Bedded soft in moss and rushes,
Safely bound with reindeer sinews;
Stilled his fretful wail by saying,
"Hush! The Naked bear will get thee!"
Lulled him into slumber, singing,
"Ewa-yea! My little owlet!
    Many things Nokomis taught him
Of the stars that shine in heaven;
Showed him Ishkoodah, the comet,
Ishkoodah, with fiery tresses;

Showed the Death-Dance of the spirits,
Warriors with their plumes and war-clubs,
Flaring far away to Northward
In the frosty nights of Winter
Showed the broad, white road in heaven,
Pathway of the ghosts, the shadows,
Running straight across the heavens,
Crowded with the ghosts, the shadows.

    At the door on Summer evenings
Sat the little Hiawatha;
Heard the whispering of the pine trees,
Heard the lapping of the water,
Sounds of music, words of wonder:
"Minne-wawa!" said the pine trees,
"Mudway-aushka! said the water.

    Saw the fire-fly, Wah-wah-taysee,
Flitting through the dusk of evening,
With the twinkle of its candle
Lighting up the brakes and bushes,
And he sang the song of children,
Sang the song Nokomis taught him:
"Wah-wah-taysee, little firefly,
Little, flitting, white-fire insect,
Little, dancing, white-fire creature,
Light me with your little candle,

Ere upon my bed I lay me,
Ere in sleep I close my eyelids!"
     Saw the moon rise from the water
Rippling, rounding from the water,
Saw the flecks and shadows on it,
Whispered, "What is that, Nokomis?"
And the good Nokomis answered:
"Once a warrior, very angry,
Seized his grandmother, and threw her
Up into the sky at midnight;
Right against the moon he threw her;
'Tis her body that you see there."
     Saw the rainbow in the heaven,
In the eastern sky, the rainbow,
"Whispered, "What is that Nokomis?"
And the good Nokomis answered:
'Tis the heaven of flowers you see there;
All the wild-flowers of the forest,
All the lilies of the prairie,
When on earth they fade and perish,
Blossom in that heaven above us.
     When he heard the owls at midnight,
Hooting, laughing in the forest,
"What is that?" he cried in terror:
"What is that?" he said, "Nokomis?"

And the good Nokomis answered:
"That is but the owl and owlet,
Talking in their native language,
Talking, scolding at each other."
        Then the little Hiawatha,
Learned of every bird its language,
Learned their names and all their secrets,
How they built their nests in Summer.
Where they hid themselves in Winter,
Talked with them whene'er he met them,
Called them "Hiawatha's Chickens."
        Of all beasts he learned the language,
Learned their names and all their secrets,
How the beavers built their lodges,
Where the squirrels hid their acorns,
How the reindeer ran so swiftly,
Why the rabbit was so timid,
Talked with them whene'er he met them,
Called them "Hiawatha's Brothers."
        Then Iagoo, the great boaster,
He the marvelous story-teller,
He the traveler and the talker,
He the friend of old Nokomis,
Made a bow for Hiawatha:
From a branch of ash he made it,

From an oak-bough made the arrows,
Tipped with flint, and winged with feathers,
And the cord he made of deer-skin.
    Then he said to Hiawatha:
"Go. my son, into the forest,
Where the red deer herd together,
Kill for us a famous roebuck,
Kill for us a deer with antlers!"
    Forth into the forest straightway
All alone walked Hiawatha
Proudly with his bow and arrows;
And the birds sang round him, o'er him,
"Do not shoot us, Hiawatha!"
Sang the Opechee, the robin,
Sang the bluebird, the Owaissa,
"Do not shoot us, Hiawatha!"
    Up the oak-tree, close beside him,
Sprang the squirrel, Adjidaumo,
In and out among the branches,
Coughed and chattered from the oak-tree,
Laughed, and said between his laughing,
"Do not shoot me, Hiawatha!"
    And the rabbit from his pathway
Leaped aside, and at a distance
Sat erect upon his haunches,

Half in fear and half in frolic,
Saying to the little hunter,
"Do not shoot me, Hiawatha!"
　　　But he heeded not, nor heard them,
For his thoughts were with the red deer;
On their tracks his eyes were fastened,
Leading downward to the river,
To the ford across the river,
And as one in slumber walked he.
Hidden in the alder bushes,
There he waited till the deer came,
Till he saw two antlers lifted,
Saw two eyes look from the thicket,
Saw two nostrils point to windward,
And a deer came down the pathway,
Flecked with leafy light and shadow.
And his heart within him fluttered,
Trembled like the leaves above him,
Like the birch-leaf palpitated,
As the deer came down the pathway.
　　　Then upon one knee uprising,
Hiawatha aimed an arrow;
Scarce a twig moved with his motion,
Scarce a leaf was stirred or rustled,
But the wary roebuck started

Stamped with all his hoofs together,
Listened with one foot uplifted,
Leaped as if to meet he arrow;
Ah! The singing, fatal arrow,
Like a wasp it buzzed and stung him!
Dead he lay there in the forest,
By the ford across the river;
Beat his timid heart no longer,
But the heart of Hiawatha
Throbbed and shouted and exulted,
As he bore the red deer homeward
And Iagoo and Nokomis
Hailed his coming with applauses.
From the red deer's hide Nokomis
Made a cloak for Hiawatha,
From the red deer's flesh Nokomis
Made a banquet in his honor.
All the village came and feasted,
All the guests praised Hiawatha,
Called him Strong-Heart, Soan-getaha!
Called him Loon-Heart, Mahn-go-taysee!

HIAWATHA AND MUDJEKEEWIS
HENRY WADSWORTH LONGFELLOW

Out of childhood into manhood
Now had grown my Hiawatha,
Skilled in all the craft of hunters,
Learned in all the lore of old men,
In all youthful sport and pastimes,
In all manly arts and labors.
      Swift of foot was Hiawatha;
He could shoot an arrow from him,
And run forward with such fleetness,
That the arrow fell behind him!
Strong of arm was Hiawatha;
He could shoot ten arrows upward,

From *The Song of Hiawatha*

Shoot them with such strength and swiftness,
That the tenth had left the bow-string
Ere the first to earth had fallen!
　　　He had mittens, Minjekahwun,
Magic mittens made of deer-skin;
When upon his hands he wore them,
He could smite the rocks asunder,
He could grind them into powder.
He had moccasins enchanted,
Magic moccasins of deer-skin;
When he bound them round his ankles.
When upon his feet he tied them,
At each stride a mile he measured!
　　　Much he questioned old Nokomis
Of his father Mudjekeewis;
Learned from her the fatal secret
Of the beauty of his mother,
Of the falsehood of his father;
And his heart was hot within him.
Like a living coal his heart was.
Then he said to old Nokomis,
"I will go to Mudjekeewis,
See how fares it with my father,
At the doorways of the West-Wind,
At the portals of the Sunset!"

From his lodge went Hiawatha,
Dressed for travel, armed for hunting;
Dressed in deer-skin shirt and leggings,
Richly wrought with quills and wampum;
On his head his eagle-feathers,
Round his waist his belt of wampum,
In his hand his bow of ash-wood,
Strung with sinews of the reindeer;
In his quiver oaken arrows,
Tipped with jasper, winged with feathers;
With his mittens, Minjekahwun,
With his moccasins enchanted.

Warning said the old Nokomis,
"Go not forth, O Hiawatha!
To the kingdom of the West-Wind,
To the realms of Mudjekeewis,
Lest he harm you with his magic,
Lest he kill you with his cunning!"

But the fearless Hiawatha
Heeded not her woman's warning;
Forth he strode into the forest,
At each stride a mile he measured;
Lurid seemed the sky above him,
Lurid seemed the earth beneath him,
Hot and close the air around him,

Filled with smoke and fiery vapors,
As of burning woods and prairies,
For his heart was hot within him,
Like a living coal his heart was.
　　　So he journeyed westward, westward,
Left the fleetest deer behind him,
Left the antelope and bison;
Crossed the rushing Esconaba,
Crossed the mighty Mississippi,
Passed the Mountains of the prairie,
Passed the land of Crows and Foxes,
Passed the dwellings of the Blackfeet,
Came unto the Rocky Mountains,
To the kingdom of the West-Wind,
Where upon the gusty summits
Sat the ancient Mudjekeewis,
Ruler of the winds of heaven.
　　　Filled with awe was Hiawatha
At the aspect of his father.
On the air about him wildly
Tossed and streamed his cloudy tresses,
Gleamed like drifting snow his tresses,
Glared like Ishkoodah, the comet,
Like the star with fiery tresses.
　　　Filled with joy was Mudjekeewis

When he looked on Hiawatha,
Saw his youth rise up before him
In the face of Hiawatha,
Saw the beauty of Wenonah
From the grave rise up before him.

　　"Welcome!" said he, "Hiawatha,
To the kingdom of the West-Wind!
Long have I been waiting for you!
Youth is lovely, age is lonely,
Youth is fiery, age is frosty;
You bring back the days departed,
You bring back my youth of passion,
And the beautiful Wenonah.!"

　　Many days they talked together,
Questioned, listened, waited, answered;
Much the mighty Mudjekeewis
Boasted of his ancient prowess,
Of his perilous adventures,
His indomitable courage,
His invulnerable body.

　　Patiently sat Hiawatha,
Listening to his father's boasting;
With a smile he sat and listened,
Uttered neither threat nor menace,
Neither word nor look betrayed him,

But his heart was hot within him,
Like a living coal his heart was.
        Then he said, "O Mudjekeewis,
Is there nothing that can harm you?
Nothing that you are afraid of?"
And the mighty Mudjekeewis,
Grand and gracious in his boasting,
Answered, saying, "There is nothing,
Nothing but the black rock yonder,
Nothing but the fatal Wawbeek!"
        And he looked at Hiawatha
With a wise look and benignant,
With a countenance paternal,
Looked with pride upon the beauty
Of his tall and graceful figure,
Saying "O my Hiawatha!
Is there anything can harm you?
Anything you are afraid of?"
        But the wary Hiawatha
Paused awhile, as if uncertain,
Held his peace, as if resolving,
And then answered "There is nothing,
Nothing but the bulrush yonder,
Nothing but the great Apukwa!"
        And as Mudjekeewis, rising,

Stretched his hand to pluck the bulrush,
Hiawatha cried in terror,
Cried in Well-dissembled terror,
"Kago! kago! Do not touch it!"
"Ah, kaween!" said Mudjekeewis,
"No indeed, I will not touch it!"
Then they talked of other matters;
First of Hiawatha's brothers,
First of Wabun, of the East-Wind,
Of the South-Wind, Shawondasee,
Of the North, Kabibonokka;
Then of Hiawtha's mother,
Of the beautiful Wenonah.
Of her birth upon the meadow,
Of her death, as old Nokomis
Had remembered and related.

    And he cried, "O Mudjekeewis,
It was you who killed Wenonah,
Took her young life and her beauty,
Broke the Lily of the Prairie,
Trampled it beneath your footsteps;
You confess it! You confess it!"
And the mighty Mudjekeewis
Tossed upon the wind his tresses,
Bowed his hoary head in anguish,

With a silent nod assented.
       Then up started Hiawatha,
And with threatening look and gesture
Laid his hand upon the black rock,
On the fatal Wabeek laid it,
With his mittens, Minjekahwun,
Rent the cutting jag asunder,
Smote and crushed it into fragments,
Hurled them madly at his father,
The remorseful Mudjekeewis,
For his heart was hot within him,
Like a living coal his heart was.
       But the ruler of the West-Wind
Blew the fragments backward from him,
With the breathing of his nostrils,
With the tempest of his anger,
Blew them back at his assailant;
Seized the bulrush, the Apukwa,
Dragged it with its roots and fibres
From the margin of the meadow,
From its ooze the giant bulrush;
Long and loud laughed Hiawatha!
Then began the deadly conflict,
Hand to hand among the mountains;
From his eyry screamed the eagle,

The Keneu, the great war-eagle,
Sat upon the crags around them,
Wheeling flapped his wings above them.
　　　Like a tall tree in the tempest
Bent and lashed the giant bulrush;
And in masses huge and heavy
Crashing fell the fatal Wawbeek;
Till the earth shook with the tumult
And confusion of the battle,
And the air was full of shoutings,
And the thunder of the mountains,
Starting, answered, "Baim-wawa!"
　　　Back retreated Mudjekeewis,
Rushing westward o'er the mountains,
Stumbling westward down the mountains,
Three whole days retreated fighting,
Still pursued by Hiawatha
To the doorways of the West-Wind,
To the portals of the Sunset,
To the earth's remotest border,
Where into the empty spaces
Sinks the sun, as a flamingo
Drops into her nest at nightfall
In the melancholy marshes.
　　　"Hold!" at length cried Mudjekeewis,

"Hold, my son, my Hiawatha!
'T'is impossible to kill me,
For you cannot kill the immortal.
I have put you to this trial,
But to know and prove your courage;
Now receive the prize of valor!

"Go back to your home and people,
Live among them, toil among them,
Cleanse the earth from all that harms it,
Clear the fishing-grounds and rivers,
Slay all monsters and magicians,
All the Wendigoes, the giants,
All the serpents, the Kenabeeks,
As I slew the Mishe-Mokwa,
Slew the Great Bear of the mountains.

"And at last, when Death draws near you,
When the awful eyes of Pauguk
Glare upon you in the darkness,
I will share my kingdom with you,
Ruler shall you be thenceforward
Of the Northwest-Wind, Keewaydin,
Of the home-wind, the Keewaydin."

Thus was fought that famous battle
In the dreadful days of Shah-shah,
In the days long since departed,

In the kingdom of the West-Wind.
Still the hunter sees its traces
Scattered far o'er hill and valley;
Sees the giant bulrush growing
By the ponds and water-courses,
Sees the masses of the Wawbeek
Lying still in every valley.

     Homeward now went Hiawatha;
Pleasant was the landscape round him,
Pleasant was the air above him,
For the bitterness of anger
Had departed wholly from him,
From his brain the thought of vengeance,
From his heart the burning fever.

     Only once his pace he slackened,
Only once he paused or halted,
Paused to purchase heads of arrows
Of the ancient Arrow-maker,
In the land of the Dacotahs,
Where the Falls of Minnehaha
Flash and gleam among the oak-trees,
Laugh and leap into the valet.

     There the ancient Arrow-maker
Made his arrow-heads of sandstone,
Arrow-heads of chalcedony,

Arrow-heads of flint and jasper,
Smoothed and sharpened at the edges,
Hard and polished, keen and costly.
　　　With him dwelt his dark-eyed daughter,
Wayward as the Minnehaha,
With her moods of shade and sunshine,
Eyes that smiled and frowned alternate,
Feet as rapid as the river,
Tresses flowing like the water,
And as musical a laughter:
And he named her from the river,
From the water-fall he named,
Minnehaha, Laughing Water.
　　　Was it then for heads of arrows,
Arrow-heads of chalcedony,
Arrow-heads of flint and jasper,
That my Hiawatha halted
In the land of the Dakotahs?
　　　Was it not to see the maiden,
See the face of Laughing Water
Peeping from behind the curtain,
Hear the rustling of her garments
From behind the waving curtain,
As one sees the Minnehaha
Gleaming, glancing through the branches.

As one hears the Laughing Water
From behind its screen of branches?
　　　　Who shall say what thoughts and visions
Fill the fiery brains of young men?
Who shall say what dreams of beauty
Filled the heart of Hiawatha?
All he told to old Nokomis,
When he reached the lodge at sunset,
Was the meeting with is father,
Was his fight with Mudjekeewis,
Not a word he said of arrows,
Not a word of Laughing Water.

Indian Mermaids and Fairies
Charles M. Skinner

The Indians are a serious people; but while their symbols and fictions contain much that repels civilized imagination, much of killing, fighting, and robbery, they have many of the gentler sort, and some are absolute poetry. Students of their myths are sure to be impressed, before they have carried their research far, with the likeness of some of these legends to the traditions that have come to us from Greece, from Israel, from Egypt, and from India. There is, for example, a myth that is prevalent over half the world, if not the whole of it, in which a person is translated from his element into either water, air, or fire, and usually seeks to draw others after him, either by force or love. We have stories of mermen and mermaids, firmly believed by nav-

igators of the South Seas, and more doubted by Columbus than he doubted his vane or his needle. We have tales of tritons, nymphs, and sirens from the Greek; Undine and Melusina are types of somewhat later date; and no longer ago than 1782 one Venant St. Germain reported that he had seen a mermaid on Lake Superior at the south end of the Paté. It was the size of a seven-year-old child, brown of skin and wooly as to hair. He wanted to shoot it, but the Indians who were rowing his canoe, cried in alarm, that it was a water-god, and if injured would fearfully revenge itself. Apparently it had read the thought of the adventurer, or had learned to know a rifle when it saw one, for within a couple of hours a storm broke, and for three days there was a downpour with violent gales.

An Alaskan tribe tells that it crossed the sea under the lead of a man-fish, with green hair and beard, who charmed the whole company with his singing.

The Canadian Indians relate that a member of the Ottawa tribe, while lounging beside a stream, was confronted by an undoubted mermaid that arose through the water and begged him to help her to the land. Her long hair hung dripping over her shoulders, her blue eyes looked pleadingly into his. Would he not take her to his people? She was weary of being half a fish and wanted to be all human, but this might be only if she was wedded. The Ottawa, moved by her appeal, took her home doubtless in his arms, for the substitution of

fish-tails for feet would have been a sore hindrance in walking through the woods. He adopted her, found a husband for her, in time—an Adirondack youth—and on their marriage the dusky Undine received a soul. But the people did not like her. They held her in distrust. In the end the Ottawas and Adirondacks fought about her. Their war continued until all of the latter tribe had perished; all save one, who, wandering beside the Mississippi at St. Anthony's falls, into which she had been thrown by her vexed and vexatious relatives-in-law, was seen by her and pulled beneath the water to her home; for she had become a mermaid once more. The Minnesota lumbermen have made the river so turbid that one seldom sees her nowadays.

Battao, a Nisqually girl, of Puget Sound, was plagued by lovers. She had charm and gentleness, and she had prospects, and it was the latter that kept her suitors hanging about the premises; for her father was rich in dogs, boats, arms, skins, and ornaments, and fathers cannot live forever. Battao was kind to these gentlemen, though she could not help yawning in the middle of their most impassioned declarations—they were such old stories. There came to the village, one summer, a tall stranger, of noble presence, who had been far beyond the mountains and far beyond the sea. He had tales to tell of other lands, and sights and adventures so strange that even the old medicine-man forgot himself and listened

with the same breathless interest as did the boy at his feet. To Battao this stranger stood for all that was daring and splendid. She was touched by a new emotion. She admired him. She was restless when he was absent, happy when he was near. On a morning when a warm, luminous mist hung over the sound, the stranger, who had been strolling and talking with her, looked into her face with a smile, then, without further word, walked off on the surface of the water toward Fox Island, and disappeared in the fog. The girl was naturally startled and frightened; and as day after day went by and he did not return, a sadness weighed upon her which she tried to dissipate by visits to the island. Every morning she would be rowed across from the mainland, where she lived, and there she would sit, hours together, running beach-sand and pebbles through her fingers, just as she had done a thousand times during their talks. As she watched the sea with longing eyes the agates sifted out fell in the odd forms which visitors to the island have noticed. On one of these excursions her boat came to a sudden stop, as if it had been driven into mud. The oarsmen made the water foam with their paddles, but the canoe advanced not a foot. Leaning over the side to discover the cause of this detention, Battao saw the smiling face of her lover through the clear tide, far below; saw his arms outstretched to embrace her, and his voice came faint, telling her that he could not return to land, but begging her to join him

and be happy in his splendid caves. She hesitated. She tried to persuade herself into doubts. It might be a phantom that called and beckoned. But at last she bade the rowers put back and tell her father that she would return in five days; then, in an access of longing, she spread her arms and leaped into the water. There were loud lamentings as the liberated canoe returned to land, for the boatmen believed they should never see her nevermore. Great, then, was the gladness of all her people when, on the fifth day from her seeming death, she arose, radiant, from the sound, and ran up the beach to her father's lodge. In five days she returned to the sea; and from that time for several years, she divided her years between her lover and her people. She was enchanted now; more gentle, more beautiful than ever, more affectionate and thoughtful withal, for if a storm were arising, or a mishap threatened, she would appear from the waves and cry a warning. But when all of her friends had died, the ties of earth no longer held her, and she went beneath the sea to live in joy forever.

It is at the Great Lakes that we discover a complement to this tale. Near what is now Gros Carp, Michigan, lived the hunter Kandawagonosh, with his aged father and mother. Heavy were their hearts on the day when his canoe washed ashore and was found broken among the rocks; for by this token they knew he was at the bottom of the lake—the cold, unsounded water that never gave up its dead. Yet in love and

the hope of a spirit's freedom they built a memorial grave for him, and under its roof placed his knife, arrows, bow, kettle, and paint, also burying his dog alive, so that if his soul did return it would find the outfit for the journey to the happy hunting-grounds, and would guess how the old couple had lamented. The weapons and kettle were not disturbed, and in due time the old people took their way to the shadow-land together. Kandawagonosh remained at the bottom of the lake—but not dead. A water-spirit had seen and loved him. It was she who broke his canoe and drew him down, down to the grottos of crystal and green below; she who inflamed his heart with an equal love, and kept him there in a long content. Kandawagonosh had not forgotten the upper-world, however. He remembered, with moments of longing, the friends in his village, and he had misgivings when he pictured his parents weak and old. There were twinges almost like jealousy as he thought of his place being taken by others, of his name being forgotten among those who had often spoken it. Ah, yes; he wanted his freedom. He wearied of constant happiness. "Let me go back to the earth for a day and see my parents," he pleaded. "They will need my help; for winter is coming on again, and they are growing feeble." "You shall go back to sun-light for a time," consented the mermaid. "We will wait for you, our children and I. Look: here is a box of bark. Keep it always fast to your belt and bring it back, unopened. If you

take off the cover you will never see this home in the green water-world again. They embraced, and the man arose swiftly through the lake. Brighter and brighter it grew, until at last his head was above the surface and he saw once more the wooded shores and the blue sky and felt the burn of the sun. In a few strokes he reached the land. His way of breathing changed so that he could inhale air again, and he stood long on the rocks in an abandon of delight at being once more in the world of men. Of men? His parents—were they still alive? He parted the branches and plunged into the wood. He could not remember trees of such size, or in such groupings. Strange! Where his people had camped there was not so much as a clearing. Where his father's tepee had stood a pine of several years' growth moved its arms and whispered in the wind. And what was this? A grave? He bent close, for there was a sudden cloud on his sight, and examined the symbols and the weapons that were half buried in the mould. The grave was his own! Hark! What was that? Somewhere down in the earth an animal was scratching and whining. It sounded like a dog. Puzzled and troubled he sank upon the mound, and while brooding on these changes he unconsciously turned in his fingers the box his water-wife had made. The cover came off. A cloud poured from it in the shape of the mermaid, who looked at him with reproach and sorrow in her face. He sprang up and tried to embrace the vision; but it melted into air, before he

could touch it. His cry of remorse had hardly ceased when his dog burst, panting, from the grave, seized him by the throat, and forced him beneath the ground. For, without knowing it, he had been in the water for a life-time; and when he sat upon the grave all those years together had fallen upon him in an instant, and he was too old to live.

Among the great dunes, Les Grandes Sables, on the south shore of Lake Superior, lived the pukwujininee, the Indian fairies—playful, roguish, good-natured folk, who loved to prank about in the moonlight and who, if too closely watched by the fishermen off-shore, would scamper in to the spirit-wood and disappear. Often their footprints were found in the sand, marks that might have been made by the feet of little children; and on warm, still days in early autumn the hunter resting beneath a pine heard high voices, babbling merrily or singing. He said to himself it was the bees or the flies, for on such days, as you drowse at a wood's edge, you shall hear those insect voices, musical, gentle, mysterious, telling secrets you may never learn. But it was not bees or flies the Indian heard; it was the pukwujininee. He knew it when he roused from his nap and heard the snickering in the leaves; for they had plucked a feather from his hair, they had unwinged his arrows, they had pilfered a piece of skin from his coat, they had stained with a plant-juice the haunch of venison he was

carrying home. Leelinaw, daughter of a chief who lived in the dune country, was fond of lonely walks. She knew things about the trees, the rocks, the insects, and the stars that were not known to the medicine-men; and with eyes a-dream, in simple trust, she would venture into places where the hunters dared not go. Once she was absent from the village all day, and on her return in the evening told of strange people, like children who had taken her with them into the heart of the forest and sang and danced and fed her on new and delicate food. In the darkness of that night her father walked long beside the waves, and her mother gave herself to tears; for both feared that Leelinaw had been with the pukwujininee and had been made as one of themselves. If so, she would never marry with the tribe. Their anxiety did not grow less with years. She remained small and slender, with feet that fitted into the prints which were left on the sands at night; and her bright, innocent eyes were often turned to the sky or across the great water, and she would be absorbed in thought. She did not cry with admiration when hunters returned with deer. She lived on maize and roots and fruit, and was often found seated on the turf, talking to the squirrels and woodchucks, plaiting strands of her hair for nests and giving them to waiting birds, feeding honey to the butteflies, or whispering to the flowers and trees. People laughed when she declared, with an angry flush, that the animals had as good a right to live as they

did, or the Master of Life would not have made them; and that
the shedding of the blood of one another by men was folly, so
long as they had room enough in which to live apart, at peace.
And her parents sorrowed afresh, for only the pukwujininee
could be such heretics. She often spoke of the sand-hills that
were far away, under the sunset—hills like the dunes, but
higher and bright in ceaseless sunshine and a fadeless carpet
of flowers. There never was crying nor fighting nor trouble
among those hills; no hunting, no death; only love and kindness, and she longed to go there. The little people she had
seen in the wood—they might be messengers from that land.
Puzzled by such fancies, the people did as people always do
with ideas beyond their minds; laughed at them. So she
learned to hold her peace, and lived more to herself than ever.
Though in stature she remained a child, her beauty and gentleness touched the heart of one young hunter, and he sued for
her hand, albeit he had some doubt if she would make the best
of housekeepers; for as she did not eat meat she might spoil
his in the cooking. Her father, hoping that marriage would
break her of dreaming with open eyes, bring her to her senses,
and release her from the spell that had been cast on her in the
spirit world, consented—which in Indian is equivalent to com-
manded—and the girl was arrayed for the bridal. She dressed
in her finest clothes, with many embroideries of shells and
quills, braided her hair, put wild flowers in it, and gathered a

bouquet of blossoms and pine tree sprays. All declared that so pretty a bride was never seen before in the dune country, and her parents embraced her proudly. She asked the leave of all to take one more walk alone in her old playground near the wood, and the permission was given with a caution to return early. She never returned. A fisherman had seen one of the pukwujininee come out of the wood—he claimed even to recognize him in the twilight as the Fairy of the Green Pines, the tallest of his tribe—and lead the maiden tenderly away. Pine plumes nodded on his head, and he placed a spray of them in his bride's hair. They have gone to the far sand-hills, the people say.

THE RESCUE OF MOLLY FINNEY
CHARLES M. SKINNER

In 1776 Thomas Mains had cleared some acres in what is now Freeport, Maine, and had put up a comfortable log house; but he was not to enjoy his possession long. The Indians came to the place in the night, slew him and one of his children, and carried into captivity his sister-in-law, the pretty, pert, and lively Molly Finney. One of the red raiders had been shot, and on the six-weeks' march to Quebec, where the band was to collect the bounty offered by the French for the English and Yankee scalps and where they expected to sell their captive, the girl was forced to serve as nurse to the wounded man. It is thought that she put more salt and tobacco than emollients into the dressings, for the patient

would spring from his couch with the most awful howls and threaten her with beatings; but the others always interfered, for they were forced to admire her pluck and pride, albeit they told her that if the injured one died on the journey they would surely make an end of her at the same time.

On reaching Quebec she was sold to a man named Lemoine, who treated her fairly, except that he gave her no more liberty than she needed for the sweeping of dust from the walks, under his eye—and into it, when she could. She was a good cook and manager, hence she presently reached a place in the kitchen, and was there seen by one Master Beauvais, a soft-hearted, none-too stout-hearted neighbor, who found frequent reason for calls on the Lemoines, and who presently began open court to the red-cheeked wench.

Old Lemoine did not like this. An elderly wife of acid temper had suspected him of pinching the cheek of their house-maid; but be that as it might, the old fellow had paid hard cash for Molly, and the servant question was as much of a problem then as it has often been since. He was not going to let his prize escape; and biding the time when she might be trusted abroad on errands, he kept close watch upon her and locked her into her room every night. This precaution was to her ultimate advantage. One morning she answered a knock at the front door and was confronted by a young, well-appearing Yankee sea-captain whose ship had recently come to port

for trading; for hostilities were over and the colonists were eager to make money again. Before she could ask his errand—a commonplace one made up for the occasion—he had thrust a note into her hand with a sign of caution. This paper she read in her room. It told her that friends in Maine had commissioned the bearer to smuggle her away from Quebec as quickly and secretly as possible. He had learned, through diplomatic inquiry, where she was, and how closely guarded, so he would await her reply at seven o'clock next morning. At that hour she was industriously sweeping the walk, and one of the things that was swept almost into the hands of Captain McLellan as he strolled past was a folded letter, which that worthy read as soon as he had rounded the corner; for old Lemoine was glaring upon them both from the doorway. It revealed the plan of the house, showed the position of Molly's room, and appointed eleven o'clock that night as the time for escape. Prompt at the hour the sailor was under her window. He tossed a rope to her, which she made fast to her bed and descended into his arms. In a quarter of an hour the two were aboard the "Hepzibah Strong," which was off for her home port, Falmouth, at daybreak. And after the journey, of course they were married.

When Daddy Lemoine unlocked Molly's door in the morning he knocked and called, but there was no response. He entered. Gone! Ha! a note! What was that? "Woman's will

is the Lord's will. Good day, M. Lemoine." A rope, too, the minx! An elopement; that's what it was. That sneaking scamp Beauvais, with his soft voice and smooth ways! Lemoine seized his cane,—and a good stout timber it was. He went around to neighbor Beauvais, and before that worthy could offer any protest or explanation he had given him a dreadful basting.

A TRAVELLED NARRATIVE
CHARLES M. SKINNER

There is one narrative, formerly common in school-readers, in collections of moral tales for youth, and in the miscellany columns of newspapers, that is thought to have been a favorite of Aristophanes and to have beguiled the Pharaohs when they had the blues—supposing blues to have been invented in their time. Every now and again it reappears in the periodicals and enjoys a new vogue for a couple of months. Many villagers clamor for recognition as the scene of the incident, but as Rutland, Vermont makes a special appeal, it may as well have happened there as anywhere. So let it be in Rutland that the cross-roads store-keeper dwelt who was burdened by the usual loungers that sat about his

shop, talked politics, squirted tobacco-juice on his stove, and, merely to beguile the time, nibbled at his dried fish, cheese, crackers, maple sugar, and spruce gum, consuming in the course of a year a long hundredweight of these commodities. These pickings were made openly and were not looked upon as thefts any more than are the little pieces of cloth that are taken home as samples by women who go shopping. Groceries that were not nailed up—or down—were a sort of bait to gather purchasers. The store-keeper did not mind these abstractions, because he added a penny to a bill now and then, and so kept even. What he did object to was the sneaking away of dearer commodities, like white sugar, drugs, tobacco, ammunition, ribbons, boots, scented soap, and catechisms.

On a sharp night in December the usual worthies sat about the stove, telling one another how many different kinds of a great man Andrew Jackson was and what was the best way to cure mange in dogs. The air of the shop was close and hot, but those who breathed it believed it pleasanter than the crisp cold outside. Fresh and wholesome air is never so little prized as where there is most of it. The proprietor, who occupied a rickety arm-chair and was throwing in his wisdom to make the aggregate impressive, kept his eye roving over his stock, and presently he noticed that Ichabod Thompson, a shiftless, out-at-elbows fellow, was nibbling more freely from the cracker barrel than it was "genteel" to do. He pretended

ignorance of this, and in a little time he saw Ichabod slip a pat of butter out of a firkin where each pound lay neatly wrapped in cloth, take off his hat in a pretence of wiping his forehead, drop the butter into the hat, and put it on again. Ichabod then loitered ostentatiously before the harness and blanket departments, made a casual inquiry as to current rates for Dr. Pilgarlic's Providential Pills, went to the stove, spreading his hands for a moment of warmth, then, turning up his collar, said he guessed he must be going.

"Oh, don't go yet." said the shop-keeper, kindly. "Sit down a minute while I tell you what happened to Hank Buffum's big sow last week."

Not wishing to come under suspicion by exhibiting anxiety to reach home,—the place to which he never went until all the other places were closed,—Ichabod accepted a seat in the circle. The shop-keeper spun his yarns to a tenuous length. He piled wood into the stove, too, until the iron sides of it glowed cherry-red; the heat became furious, a glistening yellow streak appeared on the suspect's forehead. He wiped it away with his handkerchief. He did not seem at ease. In a few minutes he yawned, laboriously, remarked that he had been up late the night before, and that he must be going home.

"All right," consented the merchant; "but just wait a few minutes till I put up a few ginger-snaps for your missus— some I just got from Boston."

Naturally an offer like that could not be refused. It took an unconscionable time to put up a dozen little cakes, and Ichabod was now sweating butter in good earnest. He accepted the gift thankfully, yet with a certain preoccupation, and as he bent over to tuck his trousers into his boots he showed his hair soaking with grease, his collar limp with it, streaks and spatters down his coat, and spots appearing in his hat. The store-keeper winked at the members of his congress, pointed significantly to the butter-tub, then to Ichabod's hat, then laid his finger on his lips. The loungers caught the idea. and when their victim was again ready to start they remembered errands and business for him that kept him for several minutes longer in their company. The butter was now coming down in drops and rills, and the old scamp was at one moment red with heat and confusion then pale with fear, because thieves fared badly in that town. On one pretext and another he was detained till the butter was all melted and his clothes, partial ruins before, were wholly spoiled. He arose with decision at last and said he could not stay another minute. "Well," said the shop-keeper, "we can let you go now. We've had fun enough out of you to pay for the butter you stole. You'll be needing new clothes tomorrow. Give us a call. Good-night."

Rip Van WinkLe
Washington Irving

Whoever has made a voyage up the Hudson must remember the Kaatskill mountains. They are a dismembered branch of the great Appalachian family, and are seen away to the west of the river, swelling up to a noble height, and lording it over the surrounding country. Every change of season, every change of weather, indeed, every hour of the day, produces some changes in the magical hues and shapes of these mountains, and they are regarded by all the good wives, far and near, as perfect barometers. When the weather is fair and settled, they are clothed in blue and purple, and print their bold outlines on the clear evening sky;

---

* *A Posthumous Writing of Diedrich Knickerbocker.* Diedrich Knickerbocker was the imaginary character who supposedly wrote Washington Irving's *History of New York.*

but sometimes, when the rest of the landscape is cloudless, they will gather a hood of gray vapors about their summits, which, in the last rays of the setting sun, will glow and light up like a crown of glory.

At the foot of these fairy mountains, the voyager must have descried the light smoke curling up from a village, whose shingle-roofs gleam among the trees, just where the blue tints of the upland melt away into the fresh green of the nearer landscape. It is a little village, of great antiquity, having been founded by some of the Dutch colonists in the early times of the province, just about the beginning of the government of the good Peter Stuveysant, (may he rest in peace!) and there were some of the houses of the original settlers standing within a few years, built of small yellow bricks brought from Holland, having latticed windows and gable fronts, surmounted with weathercocks.

In that same village, and in one of these very houses (which, to tell the precise truth, was sadly time-worn and weather-beaten), there lived, many years since, while the country was yet a province of Great Britain, a simple, good-natured fellow, of the name of Rip Van Winkle. We was a descendant of the Van Winkles who figured so gallantly in the chivalrous days of Peter Stuyvesant, and accompanied him to the siege of Fort Christina. He inherited, however, but little of the martial character of his ancestors. I have observed that he

was a simple, good-natured man; he was, moreover, a kind neighbor, and an obedient, hen-pecked husband. Indeed, to the latter circumstance might be owing that meekness of spirit which gained him such universal popularity; for those men are most apt to be obsequious and conciliating abroad, who are under the discipline of shrews at home. Their tempers, doubtless, are rendered pliant and malleable in the fiery furnace of domestic tribulation; and a curtain-lecture is worth all the sermons in the world for teaching the virtues of patience and long-suffering. A termagant wife may, therefore, in some respects, be considered a tolerable blessing; and if so, Rip Van Winkle was thrice blessed.

Certain it is, that he was a great favorite among all the good wives of the village, who, as usual with the amiable sex, took his part in all family squabbles; and never failed, whenever they talked those matters over in their evening gossipings, to lay all the blame on Dame Van Winkle. The children of the village, too, would shout with joy whenever he approached. He assisted at their sports, made their playthings, taught them to fly kites and shoot marbles, and told them long stories of ghosts, witches, and Indians. Whenever he went dodging about the village, he was surrounded by a troop of them, hanging on his skirts, clambering on his back, and playing a thousand tricks on him with impunity; and not a dog would bark at him throughout the neighborhood.

The great error in Rip's composition was an insuperable aversion to all kinds of profitable labor. It could not be from the want of assiduity or perseverance; for he would sit on a wet rock, with a rod as long and heavy as a Tartar's lance, and fish all day without a murmur, even though he should not be encouraged by a single nibble. He would carry a fowling-piece on his shoulder for hours together, trudging through woods and swamps, and up hill and down dale, to shoot a few squirrels or wild pigeons. He would never refuse to assist a neighbor even in the roughest toil, and was a foremost man at all country frolics for husking corn, or building stone fences; the women of the village, too, used to employ him to run their errands, and to do such little jobs as their less obliging husbands would not do for them. In a word, Rip was ready to attend to anybody's business but his own; but as to doing family duty, and keeping his farm in order, he found it impossible.

In fact, he declared it was of no use to work on his farm; it was the most pestilent little piece of ground in the whole country; everything about it went wrong, and would go wrong in spite of him. His fences were continually falling to pieces; his cow would either go astray, or get among the cabbages; weeds were sure to grow quicker in his fields than anywhere else; the rain always made a point of setting in just as he had some out-door work to do; so that though his patrimonial estate had dwindled away under his management, acre by

acre, until there was little more left than a mere patch of Indian corn and potatoes, yet it was the worst conditioned farm in the neighborhood.

His children too, were as ragged and wild as if they belonged to nobody. His son, Rip, an urchin begotten in his own likeness, promised to inherit the habits, with the old clothes, of his father. He was generally seen trooping like a colt at his mother's heels, equipped in a pair of his father's cast-off galligaskins, which he had much ado to hold up with one hand, as a fine lady does her train in bad weather.

Rip Van Winkle, however, was one of those happy mortals, of foolish well-oiled dispositions, who take the world easy, eat white bread or brown, whichever can be got with least thought or trouble, and would rather starve on a penny than work for a pound. If left to himself, he would have whistled life away in perfect contentment; but his wife kept continually dinning in his ears about his idleness, his carelessness, and the ruin he was bringing on his family. Morning, noon, and night, her tongue was incessantly going, and everything he said or did was sure to produce a torrent of household eloquence. Rip had but one way of replying to all lectures of the kind, and that, by frequent use, had grown into a habit. He shrugged his shoulders, shook his head, cast up his eyes, but said nothing. This, however, always provoked a fresh volley from his wife; so that he was fain to draw off his forces, and

take to the outside of the house—the only side which, in truth, belongs to a hen-pecked husband.

Rip's sole domestic adherent was his dog Wolf, who was as much hen-pecked as his master; for Dame Van Winkle regarded them as companions in idleness, and even looked upon Wolf with an evil eye, as the cause of his master's going so often astray. True it is, in all points of spirit befitting an honorable dog, he was as courageous an animal as ever scoured the woods; but what courage can withstand the ever-enduring and all-besetting terrors of a woman's tongue? The moment Wolf entered the house his crest fell, his tail drooped to the ground, or curled between his legs, he sneaked about with a gallows air, casting many a sidelong glance at Dame Van Winkle, and at the least flourish of a broomstick or ladle he would fly to the door with yelping precipitation.

Times grew worse and worse with Rip Van Winkle as years of matrimony rolled on; a tart temper never mellows with age, and a sharp tongue is the only edged tool that grows keener with constant use. For a long while he used to console himself, when driven from home, by frequenting a kind of perpetual club of the sages, philosophers, and other idle personages of the village, which held its sessions on a bench before a small inn, designated by a rubicund portrait of His Majesty George the Third. Here they used to sit in the shade through a long lazy summer's day, talking listlessly over village gossip or

telling endless sleepy stories about nothing. But it would have been worth any statesman's money to have heard the profound discussions that sometimes took place, when by chance an old newspaper fell into their hands from some passing traveler. How solemnly they would listen to the contents, as drawled out by Derrick Van Bummel, the schoolmaster, a dapper learned little man, who was not to be daunted by the most gigantic word in the dictionary; and how sagely they would deliberate upon public events some months after they had taken place.

The opinions of this junto were completely controlled by Nicholas Vedder, patriarch of the village, and landlord of the inn, at the door of which he took his seat from morning till night, just moving sufficiently to avoid the sun and keep in the shade of a large tree; so that the neighbors could tell the hour by his movements as accurately as by a sun-dial. It is true he was rarely heard to speak, but smoked his pipe incessantly. His adherents, however (for every great man has his adherents), perfectly understood him, and knew how to gather his opinions. When anything that was read or related displeased him, he was observed to smoke his pipe vehemently, and to send forth short, frequent, and angry puffs; but when pleased, he would inhale the smoke slowly and tranquilly, and emit it in light and placid clouds; and sometimes taking the pipe from his mouth, and letting the fragrant vapor curl about his nose,

would gravely nod his head in token of perfect approbation.

From even this stronghold, the unlikely Rip was at length routed by his termagant wife, who would suddenly break in upon the tranquility of the assemblage and call the members all to naught; nor was that august personage, Nicholas Vedder himself, sacred from the daring tongue of this terrible virago, who charged him outright with encouraging her husband in habits of idleness.

Poor Rip was at last reduced almost to despair; and his only alternative, to escape from the labor of the farm and clamor of his wife, was to take gun in hand and stroll away into the woods. Here he would sometimes seat himself at the foot of a tree, and share the contents of his wallet with Wolf, with whom he sympathized as a fellow-sufferer in persecution. "Poor Wolf," he would say, "thy mistress leads thee a dog's life of it, but never mind, my lad, whilst I live thou shalt never want a friend to stand by thee!" Wolf would wag his tail, look wistfully in his master's face, and if dogs can feel pity, I verily believe he reciprocated the sentiment with all his heart.

In a long ramble of the kind on a fine autumnal day, Rip had unconsciously scrambled to one of the highest parts of the Kaatskill mountains. He was after his favorite sport of squirrel-shooting, and the still solitudes had echoed and re-echoed with the reports of his gun. Panting and fatigued, he threw himself, late in the afternoon, on a green knoll, covered

with mountain herbage, that crowned the brow of a precipice. From an opening between the trees he could overlook all the lower country for many a mile of rich woodland. He saw at a distance the lordly Hudson, far, far below him, moving on its silent but majestic course, with the reflection of a purple cloud, or the sail of a lagging bark, here and there sleeping on its glassy bosom, and at last losing itself in the blue highlands.

On the other side he looked down into a deep mountain glen, wild, lonely, and shagged, the bottom filled with fragments from the impending cliffs, and scarcely lighted by the reflected rays of the setting sun. For some time Rip lay musing on this scene; evening was gradually advancing; the mountains began to throw their long blue shadows over the valleys; he saw that it would be dark long before he could reach the village, and he heaved a heavy sigh when he thought of encountering the terrors of Dame Van Winkle.

As he was about to descend, he heard a voice from a distance, hallooing, "Rip Van Winkle, Rip Van Winkle!" He looked around, but could see nothing but a crow winging its solitary flight across the mountains. He thought his fancy must have deceived him, and turned again to descend, when he heard the same cry ring through the still evening air: "Rip Van Winkle! Rip Van Winkle"—at the same time Wolf bristled up his back, and giving a low growl, skulked to his master's side, looking fearfully down into the glen. Rip now felt a vague

apprehension stealing over him; he looked anxiously in the same direction, and perceived a strange figure slowly toiling up the rocks, and bending under the weight of something he carried on his back. He was surprised to see any human being in this lonely and unfrequented place; but supposing it to be some one of the neighborhood in need of his assistance, he hastened down to yield it.

On nearer approach he was still more surprised at the singularity of the stranger's appearance. He was a short, square-built old fellow, with thick, bushy hair, and a grizzled beard. His dress was of the antique Dutch fashion,—a cloth jerkin strapped around the waist—several pair of breeches, the outer one of ample volume, decorated with rows of buttons down the sides, and bunches at the knees. He bore on his shoulders a stout keg, that seemed full of liquor, and made signs for Rip to approach and assist him with the load. Though rather shy and distrustful of this new acquaintance, Rip complied with his usual alacrity; and mutually relieving one another, they clambered up a narrow gully, apparently the dry bed of a mountain torrent. As they ascended, Rip every now and then heard long, rolling peals, like distant thunder, that seemed to issue out of a deep ravine, or rather cleft, between lofty rocks, toward which their rugged path conducted. He paused for an instant, but supposing it to be the muttering of one of those transient thunder-showers which often take place in mountain

heights, he proceeded. Passing through the ravine, they came to a hollow, like a small amphitheatre, surrounded by perpendicular precipices, over the brinks of which impending trees shot their branches, so that you only caught glimpses of the azure sky and the bright evening cloud. During the whole time Rip and his companion had labored on in silence; for though the former marveled greatly what could be the object of carrying a keg of liquor up this wild mountain, yet there was something strange and incomprehensible about the unknown, that inspired awe and checked familiarity.

On entering the amphitheatre, new objects of wonder presented themselves. On a level spot in the centre was a company of odd-looking personages playing at ninepins. They were dressed in a quaint, outlandish fashion; some wore short doublets, others jerkins, with long knives in their belts, and most of them had enormous breeches, of similar style with that of a guide's. Their visages, too, were peculiar: one had a large beard, broad face, and small piggish eyes; the face of another seemed to consist entirely of nose, and was surmounted by a white sugar-loaf hat, set off with a little red cock's tail. They all had beards, of various shapes and colors. There was one who seemed to be the commander. He was a stout old gentleman, with a weather-beaten countenance; he wore a laced doublet, broad belt and hanger, high crowned hat and feather, red stockings, and high-heeled shoes, with

roses in them. The whole group reminded Rip of the figures in an old Flemish painting, in the parlor of Dominie Van Shaick, the village parson, and which had been brought over from Holland at the time of the settlement.

What seemed particularly odd to Rip was, that, though these folks were evidently amusing themselves, yet they maintained the gravest faces, the most mysterious silence, and were, withal, the most melancholy party of pleasure he had ever witnessed. Nothing interrupted the stillness of the scene but the noise of the balls, which, whenever they rolled, echoed along mountains like rumbling peals of thunder.

As Rip and his companion approached them, they suddenly desisted from their play, and stared at him with such fixed, statue-like gaze, and such strange, uncouth, lack-lustre countenances, that his heart turned within him and his knees smote together. His companion now emptied the contents of the keg into large flagons, and made signs to him to wait upon the company. He obeyed with fear and trembling; they quaffed the liquor in profound silence, and then returned to their game.

By degrees Rip's awe and apprehension subsided. He even ventured, when no eye was fixed upon him, to taste the beverage, which he found had much of the flavor of excellent Hollands. He was naturally a thirsty soul, and was soon tempted to repeat the draught. One taste provoked another; and he reiterated his visits to the flagon so often that at length his

senses were overpowered, his eyes swam in his head, his head gradually declined, and he fell into a deep sleep.

On waking, he found himself on the green knoll whence he had first seen the old man of the glen. He rubbed his eyes—it was a bright sunny morning. The birds were hopping and twittering among the bushes, and the eagle was wheeling aloft, and breasting the pure mountain breeze. "Surely," thought Rip, "I have not slept here all night." He recalled the occurrences before he fell asleep. The strange man with a keg of liquor—the mountain ravine—the wild retreat among the rocks–the woe-begone party at ninepins—the flagon—"Oh! That flagon! That wicked flagon!" thought Rip, "what excuse shall I make to Dame Van Winkle?"

He looked round for his gun, but in place of the clean, well-oiled fowling-piece, he found an old firelock lying by him, the barrel encrusted with rust, the lock falling off, and the stock worm-eaten. He now suspected that the grave roisters of the mountains had put a trick upon him, and having dosed him with liquor, had robbed him of his gun. Wolf, too, had disappeared, but he might have strayed away after a squirrel or partridge. He whistled after him, and shouted his name, but all in vain; the echoes repeated his whistle and shout, but no dog was to be seen.

He determined to revisit the scene of the last evening's gambol, and if he met with any of the party, to demand his dog

and his gun. As he rose to walk, he found himself stiff in the joints, and wanting in his usual activity. "These mountain beds do not agree with me," thought Rip, "and if this frolic should lay me up with a fit of the rheumatism, I shall have a blessed time with Dame Van Winkle." With some difficulty he got down into the glen: he found the gully up which he and his companion had ascended the preceding evening; but to his astonishment a mountain stream was now foaming down it, leaping from rock to rock, and filling the glen with babbling murmurs. He, however, made sift to scramble up its sides, working his toilsome way through thickets of birch, sassafras, and witch-hazel, and sometimes tripped or entangled by the wild grape-vines that twisted their coils or tendrils from tree to tree, and spread a kind of network in his path.

At length he reached to where the ravine had opened through the cliffs to the amphitheatre; but no traces of such opening remained. The rocks presented a high, impenetrable wall, over which the torrent came tumbling in a sheet of feathery foam, and fell into a broad deep basin, black from the shadows of the surrounding forest. Here then, poor Rip was brought to a stand. He again called and whistled after his dog; he was only answered by the cawing of a flock of idle crows, sporting high in air about a dry tree that overhung a sunny precipice; and who, secure in their elevation, seemed to look down and scoff at the poor man's perplexities. What was to be

done? The morning was passing away, and Rip felt famished for want of his breakfast. He grieved to give up his dog and gun; he dreaded to meet his wife; but it would not do to starve among the mountains. He shook his head, shouldered the rusty firelock, and, with a heart full of trouble and anxiety, turned his footsteps homeward.

As he approached the village he met a number of people, but none whom he knew, which somewhat surprised him, for he had thought himself acquainted with every one in the country round. Their dress, too, was of a different fashion from that to which he was accustomed. They all stared at him with equal marks of surprise, and whenever they cast their eyes upon him, invariably stroked their chins. The constant recurrence of this gesture induced Rip, involuntarily, to do the same, when, to his astonishment, he found his beard had grown a foot long!

He had now entered the skirts of the village. A troop of strange children ran at his heels, hooting after him, and pointing at his gray beard. The dogs, too, not one of which he recognized for an old acquaintance, barked at him as he passed. The very village was altered; it was larger and more populous. There were rows of houses which he had never seen before, and those which had been his familiar haunts had disappeared. Strange names were over the doors—strange faces at the windows—everything was strange. His mind now misgave

him; he began to doubt whether both he and the world around him were not bewitched. Surely this was his native village, which he had left but the day before. There stood the Kaatskill mountains—there ran the silver Hudson at a distance—there was every hill and dale precisely as it had always been. Rip was sorely perplexed. "That flagon last night," thought he, "has addled my poor head sadly!"

It was with some difficulty that he found the way to his own house, which he approached with silent awe, expecting every moment to hear the shrill voice of Dame Van Winkle. He found the house gone to decay—the roof fallen in, the windows shattered, and the doors off the hinges. A half-starved dog that looked like Wolf was skulking about it. Rip called him by name, but the cur snarled, showed his teeth, and passed on. This was an unkind cut indeed. "My very dog," sighed poor Rip, "has forgotten me!"

He entered the house, which to tell the truth, Dame Van Winkle had always kept in neat order. It was empty, forlorn, and apparently abandoned. This desolateness overcame all his connubial fears—he called loudly for his wife and children—the lonely chambers rang for a moment with his voice, and then all again was silence.

He now hurried forth, and hastened to his old resort, the village inn, but it, too, was gone. A large rickety wooden building stood in its place, with great gaping windows, some

of them broken and mended with old hats and petticoats, and over the door was painted, "The Union Hotel, by Jonathan Doolittle." Instead of the great tree that used to shelter the quiet little Dutch inn of yore, there now was reared a tall naked pole, with something on top that looked like a red night-cap, and from it was fluttering a flag, on which was a singular assemblage of stars and stripes;—all this was strange and incomprehensible. He recognized on the sign, however, the ruby face of King George, under which he had smoked so many a peaceful pipe; but even this was singularly metamorphosed. The red coat was changed for one of blue and buff, a sword was held in the hand instead of a scepter, the head was decorated with a cocked hat, and underneath was painted in large characters, GENERAL WASHINGTON.

There was, as usual, a crowd of folk about the door, but none that Rip recollected. The very character of the people seemed changed. There was a busy, bustling, disputatious tone about it, instead of the accustomed phlegm and drowsy tranquility. He looked in vain for the sage Nicholas Vedder, and with his broad face, double chin, and fair long pipe, uttering clouds of tobacco-smoke instead of idle speeches; or Van Bummel, the schoolmaster, doling forth the contents of an ancient newspaper. In place of these, a lean, bilious-looking fellow, with his pockets full of handbills, was haranguing vehemently about rights of citizens—elections—members of

congress—liberty— Bunker's Hill—heroes of seventy-six—and other words, which were a perfect Babylonish jargon to the bewildered Van Winkle.

The appearance of Rip, with his long, grizzled beard, his rusty fowling piece, his uncouth dress, and an army of women and children at his heels, soon attracted the attention of the tavern-politicians. They crowded round him, eying him from head to foot with great curiosity. The orator bustled up to him, and, drawing him partly aside, inquired "On which side he voted?" Rip stared in vacant stupidity. Another short but busy little fellow pulled him by the arm, and, rising on tiptoe, inquired in his ear, "Whether he was Federal or Democrat?" Rip was equally at a loss to comprehend the question; when a knowing, self-important old gentleman, in a sharp cocked hat, made his way through the crowd, putting them to the right and left with his elbows as he passed, and planting himself before Van Winkle, with one arm akimbo, the other resting on his cane, his keen eyes and sharp hat penetrating, as it were, into his very soul, demanded in an austere tone, "What brought him to the election with a gun on his shoulder, and a mob at his heels; and whether he meant to breed a riot in the village?" —"Alas! Gentlemen," cried Rip, somewhat dismayed, "I am a poor quiet man, a native of the place, and a loyal subject of the King, God bless him!"

Here a general shout burst from the bystanders—"a

tory! a tory! a spy! a refugee! hustle him! Away with him!" It was with great difficulty that the self-important man in the cocked hat restored order; and, having assumed a tenfold austerity of brow, demanded again of the unknown culprit, what he came there for, and whom he was seeking? The poor man humbly assured him that he meant no harm, but merely came there in search of some of his neighbors, who used to keep about the tavern.

"Well—who are they?—name them."

Rip bethought himself a moment, and inquired, "Where's Nichoas Vedder?"

There was a silence for a little while, when a old man replied, in a thin piping voice, "Nicholas Vedder! Why, he is dead and gone these eighteen years! There was a wooden tombstone in that churchyard that used to tell all about him, but that's rotten and gone too."

"Where's Brom Dutcher?"

"Oh, he went off to the army in the beginning of the war; some say he was killed at the storming of Stony Point—others say he was drowned in a squall at the foot to Antony's Nose. I don't know—he never came back again.

"Where's Van Bummel, the schoolmaster?"

"He went off to the wars too, was a great militia general, and is now in congress."

Rip's heart died away at hearing of these sad changes

in his home and friends, and finding himself thus alone in the world. Every answer puzzled him too, by treating of such enormous lapses of time, and of matters which he could not understand: war— congress—Stony Point—he had no courage to ask after any more friends, but cried out in despair, "Does nobody here know Rip Van Winkle?"

"Oh, Rip Van Winkle!" exclaimed two or three, "Oh, to be sure! that's Rip Van Winkle yonder, leaning against the tree."

Rip looked, and he beheld a precise counterpart of himself, as he went up the mountain; apparently as lazy, and certainly as ragged. The poor fellow was now completely confounded. He doubted his own identity, and whether he was himself or another man. In the midst of his bewilderment, the man in the cocked hat demanded who he was, and what was his name.

"God knows," exclaimed he, at his wit's end; "I'm not myself—I'm somebody else—that's me yonder—no–that's somebody else got into my shoes—I was myself last night, but I fell asleep on the mountain, and they've changed my gun, and everything's changed, and I'm changed, and I can't tell what's my name, or who I am."

The bystanders now began to look at each other, nod, wink significantly, and tap their fingers against their fore-heads. There was a whisper, also, about securing the gun, and keeping the old fellow from doing mischief, at the very sug-

gestion of which the self-important man in the cocked hat retired with some precipitation. At this critical moment a fresh, comely woman pressed through the throng to get a peep at the gray-bearded man. She had a chubby child in her arms, which, frightened at his looks, began to cry. "Hush, Rip," cried she, "hush you little fool; the old man won't hurt you." The name of the child, the air of the mother, the tone of her voice, all awakened a train of recollections in his mind. "What is your name, my good woman?" asked he.

"Judith Gardenier."

"And your father's name?"

"Ah, poor man, Rip Van Winkle was his name, but it's twenty years since he went away from home with his gun, and never has been heard of since,—his dog came home without him; but whether he shot himself, or was carried away by the Indians, nobody can tell. I was then but a little girl."

Rip had but one question more to ask: but he put it with a faltering voice:

"Where's your mother?"

"Oh, she too had died but a short time since; she broke a blood vessel in a fit of passion at a New England peddler."

There was a drop of comfort, at least, in this intelligence. The honest man could contain himself no longer. He caught his daughter and her child in his arms. "I am your father!" cried he—"Young Rip Van Winkle once—old Rip Van

Winkle now!—Does nobody know poor Rip Van Winkle?"

All stood amazed, until an old woman, tottering out from among the crowd, put her hand to her brow, and peering under it in his face for a moment, exclaimed, "Sure enough! It is Rip Van Winkle—it is himself! Welcome home again, old neighbor. Why, where have you been these twenty long years?"

Rip's story was soon told, for the whole twenty years had been to him but as one night. The neighbors stared when they heard it; some were seen to wink at each other, and put their tongues in their cheeks: and the self-important man in the cocked hat, whom when the alarm was over, had returned to the field, screwed down the corners of his mouth, and shook his head—upon which there was a general shaking of the head throughout the assemblage.

It was determined, however, to take the opinion of old Peter Vanderdonk, who was seen slowly advancing up the road. He was a descendant of the historian of that name, who wrote one of the earliest accounts of the province. Peter was the most ancient inhabitant of the village, and well versed in all the wonderful events and traditions of the neighborhood. He recollected Rip at once, and corroborated his story in the most satisfactory manner. He assured the company that it was a fact, handed down from his ancestor the historian, that the Kaatskill mountains had always been haunted by strange beings. That it was affirmed that the great Hendrick Hudson,

the first discoverer of the river and country, kept a vigil there every twenty years, with his crew of the Half-moon; being permitted in this way to revisit the scenes of his enterprise, and keep a guardian eye upon the river and the great city called by his name. That his father had once seen them in their old Dutch dresses playing at ninepins in a hollow of the mountain; and that he himself had heard, one summer afternoon, the sound of their balls, like distant peals of thunder.

To make a long story short, the company broke up and retuned to the more important concerns of the election. Rip's daughter took him home to live with her; for she had a snug, well-furnished house, and a stout, cheery farmer for a husband, whom Rip recollected for one of the urchins that used to climb upon his back. As to Rip's son and heir, who was the ditto of himself, seen leaning against the tree, he was employed to work on the farm; but evinced an hereditary disposition to attend to anything else but his business.

Rip now resumed his old walks and habits; he soon found many of his former cronies, though all rather the worse for the wear and tear of time; and preferred making friends among the rising generation, with whom he soon grew into great favor.

Having nothing to do at home, and being arrived at that happy age when a man can be idle with impunity, he took his place once more on the bench at the inn-door, and was

reverenced as one of the patriarchs of the village, and a chronicle of the old times "before the war." It was some time before he could get into the regular track of gossip, or could be made to comprehend the strange events that had taken place during his torpor. How that there had been a revolutionary war,—that the country had thrown off the yoke of old England,—and that instead of being a subject of his Majesty George the Third, he was now a free citizen of the United States. Rip, in fact, was no politician; the changes of states and empires made but little impression on him; but there was one species of despotism under which he long groaned, and that was—petticoat government. Happily, that was at an end; he had got back his neck out of the yoke of matrimony, and could go in and out whenever he pleased, without dreading the tyranny of Dame Van Winkle. Whenever her name was mentioned, however, he shook his head, shrugged his shoulders, and cast up his eyes, which might pass either for an expression of resignation to his fate, or joy at his deliverance.

He used to tell his story to every stranger that arrived at Mr. Doolittle's hotel. He was observed, at first, to vary on some points every time he told it, which was doubtless, owing to his having so recently awaked. It at last settled down precisely to the tale I have related, and not a man, woman, or child in the neighborhood but knew it by heart. Some always pretended to doubt the reality of it, and insisted that Rip had been out of his

head, and that this was one point on which he always remained flighty. The old Dutch inhabitants, however, almost universally gave it full credit. Even to this day they never hear a thunderstorm of a summer afternoon about the Kaatskill, but they say Hendrick Hudson and his crew are at the game of ninepins; and it is a common wish of all hen-pecked husbands in the neighborhood, when life hangs heavy on their hands, that they might have a quieting draught out of Rip Van Winkle's flagon.

THE LONG SLEEP
CHARLES M. SKINNER

Mount Mianomo, or Rag Rock, in eastern Massachusetts, was one of the dead monsters that had crawled down from the north with ice and stones on its back to desolate the sun god's land. All of these creatures were checked when they reached the hollows dug by the sun god to stay their march—the hollows that have become the pretty New England lakes—and there the god pelted them to death with heated spears. At the foot of this hill, three centuries ago lived many of the Aberginians—progenitors, it is said of the Aber-Nits, that arose on the isle of Manhatta in after years. Their chief was one Wabanowi, who thought more of himself than all the rest of his people did, who never learned anything, never made a true prophecy, and passed into vulgar local history as Headman Stick-in-the-mud. This chief had a

daughter, Heart-stealer, and he made it a duty to nag and to thwart her in every wish, as befitted the Indian parent of romance. Fighting Bear, chief of the Narragansetts, fell in love with the girl, and after a speech of three pages on which he likened himself to the sun, the storm, the ocean, to all the strong animals he could remember, and the girl to the deer,— could it have been a dear?—the singing bird, the zephyr, the waves, and the flowers, he descended to business and claimed her hand. Every Indian, he said, had heard the prophecy that a great race with sick faces, hair on its teeth, thickly clad in summer, and speaking in a harsh tongue, was coming to drive the red man from the land of his fathers. By this marriage the Aberginians and Narragansetts would be united, and two such families could destroy anybody or anything.

The professional pride of Stick-in-the-mud was touched. He sprang to his feet and cried: "Who has foretold this? I didn't. There is only one prophet in this district, and that's me. It isn't for green youngsters, Narragansetts at that, to meddle with this second sight business. Understand? Moreover, my arm is so strong it needs no help to exterminate an enemy. I can beat him with my left hand tied behind me. Had you merely asked for my daughter I would have given her up without a struggle. If somebody doesn't take her soon I shall lose my reason. But you have added insult to oratory, and if you don't go quick you'll never get there at all."

Thus speaking, Stick-in-the-mud once more wrapped his furs around him so that only his nose and his pipe were left outside, while Fighting Bear folded his arms, scowled, observed something to the effect that Ha, ha! a time would come, and strode into the forest.

One evening a smoke hung over Rag Rock and shadowy figures flitted through it. A vague fear possessed the public. Stick-in-the-mud, waking from a mince-pie dream in the middle of the night, saw in his door, faint against the sky, the shape of a woman who beckoned, and hoping to discover some secret that would be more useful to him in his fortune-telling matches than his usual and lamentable guess-work, hearose and followed her. The spirit moved lightly, silently up Rag Rock and entered a cavern glowing with soft light and bedded with deep moss. He sank upon this cushioned floor, at a gesture from the spirit; then, with her arms waving above him, he fell into a sleep. Next day, and for several days, the citizens scoured the woods, the hills, and every other thing except themselves, in the search for Stick-in-the-mud, but they did not find him. Another man, who had enjoyed singular misfortune in foretelling the weather, was promoted to be seer; and then when the news reached Rhode Island—that was what it was going to be ere long—Fighting Bear hurried to the scene of his former interview and again claimed Heart-stealer as his bride. Nobody said a word, so he took her to his home.

Now came the men of sick and hairy faces, white men, who wanted the earth and took it, making it no longer a pleasant place to live on. It was plain that they were the people whose coming had been foretold, and when King Philip waged a war against the English, Fighting Bear and a hundred of his friends joined in the riot. He was beaten soundly, and, being a man of sense, once was enough. He kept the peace after that.

When Stick-in-the-mud awoke the cave was lighted again and the spirit that had led him there stood watching. As his eyes opened she spoke: "Wabanowi, I caused you to sleep that you might be spared the pain of seeing your people forsake their home for other lands. The men with pale faces and black hearts are here. Had you been with your people you would have stirred them to fight, and all would have been killed. As it is, they have not fought. I now set you free. Go into the Narragansett country and live with your daughter. You will find her married to Fighting Bear. Do not disturb their happiness. Come."

Then the rock opened and the chief tottered into the sunlight. He was full of rheumatism and fringed with moth-eaten whiskers that presently made the dogs bark. He needed new clothes. He needed a dinner. He needed a smoke. If he had known anything about fire-water he would have been sure that he needed a drink. He looked down at Lake Initou: not a canoe! On the site of his village: not a wigwam! The trees had been cut, log houses stood in the clearings, people

with colorless faces were using strange implements in tilled fields. A cock crew. Stick-in-the-mud started; it was a new sound to him. A horse laughed; he winced. A sheep bleated; he began to sweat. A cow lowed; he started for a tree. A jackass warbled; he looked around for the cave, but it had closed.

Descending after he had gained confidence, he shaved himself with a quohog shell, found his wreck of a canoe, guided it for the last time across the lake, and landing at its southern end crushed it to pieces—not the pond, but the canoe. Then he went to Providence, where his daughter met him and presented a few of her children, who climbed over him, hung on to his hair, and otherwise made him feel at home. He saw that he had been outclassed as a prophet and that if he had taken the advice of his son-in-law he might have avoided being put to sleep in Rag Rock. Still, this Indian Rip Van Winkle had been refreshed by his slumbers, and he lived for a long time after, spending part of every pleasant day in playing horse with the youngest of his grandchildren—for he had found that horses do not bite hard— and proudly watching the replacement of youngest No. 8 by youngest No. 9, then by No. 10, and so on to a matter of 18 or 20. In September, on the day nearest to full moon, he still goes back to Rag Rock and looks off at sunrise. You may see him then, or you may see him half an hour later skimming the surface of Horn Pond in his shadow canoe. Having thus revisited the scenes of his youth, he retires for another year.

THE GANDER'S MESSAGE
CHARLES M. SKINNER

In the eighteenth century there stood a gambrelled house at Somerset, Massachusetts, where Widow Le Doit lived with her daughter and five stout sons. Biel, the youngest, suffered a fate common to the smallest member of a family in that he was teased and badgered by his brothers so that he often begged his mother's permission to go away and earn his living elsewhere. Above all things he would be a sailor. He was a confirmed roamer, and he wanted more room. In one of is lonely rambles he caught a wild goose that he domesticated and prized until someone shot her,—he suspected his brothers,—but one of her eggs was hatched under a hen and the "cute" little gosling that emerged became a spe-

cial charge of Biel. A time came at last when the widow yielded to the boy's pleadings and consented that he should go to
sea. As a pet, a reminder of home, and possibly as a
Thanksgiving dinner in some distant port, the gander kept him
company in the ship "L'Ouverture," bound for the Western
Indies. Three years the ship was gone, for she was to change
cargoes and trade in the interests of her owners, so the letters
were infrequent. Biel might be in Uruguay, China, or Denmark,
or he might be on any of the seas.

On the third Thanksgiving day, when the horn was
blown for the great dinner of the year at the old home, a queer
call came back; the honk of a goose. Widow Le Doit's eyes
filled. She recalled her son's pry gander. Another blast and
another call from the meadow. The daughter shuddered a little
"Is the meadow haunted," she asked, "or is something about
to happen?"

"Why do you speak of such things, Annie?"

"Because there is only one wild goose in the world that
knows our horn and will answer it. Blow once more, mother."

A third blast rang from the horn and echoed against the
low hills. A form arose from the grass and the laurel patches in
the pasture and flew low toward the house. It alighted before
the two women, honked loudly, then flew off again. Annie hid
her face on her mother's shoulder. "Biel is dead!" she cried.

The elder woman soothed the younger and tried to

laugh at her fears, but the laughter had no ring in it. The two went in, presently, to receive their guests. All seemed dull and oppressed until another call of the wild goose sent a little shudder through the company. It seemed like an omen.

"It is there again!" exclaimed the widow "I will call it." And stepping to the door she sounded a stronger note than ever on the horn. In a few moments the wild fowl, as the others thought it, alighted in the yard and pattered up the walk toward the door. Annie sprang upon it and carried it to the table, where it stood stretching its wings and pluming itself, not in the least disturbed by the presence of the company, until, with a sudden rouse, as if it had heard something at a distance that it meant to answer, it stretched forth its neck and uttered a honk that made the roof ring. A step sounded on the door-stone, a brown-faced, sturdy figure dashed in, caught the widow about the waist with one arm, Annie with the other, and smacked them heartily; then gave to each of the brothers such a resounding whack upon his back that he quailed. It was Biel. After a minute of tears, laughter, and hand-shaking the gander paddled to the edge of the table and cocked up an inquiring eye. "Well, if it isn't our gander!" cried the sailor. "He cut away from the ship two days ago, and I supposed he was a long way ahead of us. Aha! I see you thought we were wrecked. Not a bit of it. Gold in our pockets and appetites for two. Am I in time for the Thanksgiving dinner?

The Golden Tooth
Charles M. Skinner

Goedevrouw Doortje Stogpens sat alone in her little back parlor in a little back street of the little town of Albany, dreaming over the pictures in a meager fire and taking comfort in the monotonous tapping of rain on the window. Her knitting lay in her lap, and she was debating within herself whether she would have more pleasure in quaffing a gill of Hollands, as a sleeping draught, or foregoing and having so much the more spirits in stock. A drink avoided was twopence saved, and the saving of twopence was a thing to be seriously debated. She finally promised herself an extra allowance at Christmas, and an extra pinch of snuff at once, as a reward for abstaining, so, with a sigh of resignation, she arose to prepare for bed: an operation that in the case of a

Dutch vrouw involved not merely the mysterious marching and countermarching, the opening and closing of doors, the moving of furniture, the overhauling of bureaus, and the displacing of dry goods in closets that is common in the ceremonies which precede retirement in Western households, but the removal of a matter of half a dozen petticoats, some of them quilted and lined with silk from China and therefore as greatly prized as family silver. Not more than four or five of these garments had been unpinned when there came a quick, low knock at the door.

"Who is there?" she asked.

"Does the wife of Diederik Stogpens, the sailor, live here?" was asked, in harsh, weather-cracked tones outside.

"Yes."

"Then, please let me in."

"I do not know your voice. Who are you that comes around at this hour?" (Here the hanging clock struck eight.)

"Do you hear that? Be off with you."

"I am a friend. I bring news of your husband."

"My husband! It's near two years since I've heard from him." The dame went eagerly to the door, just as she was, with barely four petticoats on, and drew the bolt. A burly, seafaring sort of person, with a wide head and a thick neck, entered the room, stamped his feet on the sanded floor to shake the water from his baggy trousers, and gave his wilted hat a flip that

scattered rain drops to the ceiling. A long queue dangled between his shoulders, and as he stepped into the light of her candle the goedevrouw discovered that her visitor's face was ringed with bedraggled red whiskers that had been the sport of the winds for nobody could tell how long. He lounged into Madame Stogpen's easy-chair and put his wet boots into the ashes, causing them to steam and hiss like a barbecue, and he then pulled forth a short, rank pipe, and, lighting it with a coal that he picked up in his thick, brown fingers, began to utter smoke through his whiskers, as a wood will issue after rain. "And if you have a noggin of liquor handy, ma'am," he remarked, "I could persuade myself to taste it, being that I am chilled with long travel in the wind and rain."

Poor Doortje! She wished now that she had yielded to the craving of her thirst, but there was the gin bottle in plain sight, and how could she refuse? "Never mind a cup," said the stranger. "I'm used to taking it from glass." Whereupon he tilted the nectar into his beard, and when he offered the bottle again to his hostess a miracle had been wrought, for, lo! it was empty.

"Ha! That's better," said the salt-looking person, sinking deeper into the chair, resting his head on its back, and straddling his legs farther apart. "So you are the wid—the wife of my old friend Dirk Stogpens, eh? A mad fellow, madam—a mad fellow!"

"Not at all, sir. The steadiest, most saving—"

"Tut, tut! Oh, you mean, at home? I dare say, but at sea, or in a foreign port, the deepest drinker, the loudest singer, the hardest swearer, the quickest fighter, the longest at cards, the quickest to see a pretty—hm! Eh, him!" And the stranger cleared his throat.

"You are wrong, I'm sure. Most likely it is some other Stogpens. Now, there's a branch of our family in Weehawk."

"No, for he gave me your address before he left our ship to overhaul a rich-looking stranger on the Grand Banks."

"Overhaul?"

"Aye. To board her—to capture—to loot—you understand."

"To capture? But there is no war."

"Haw, haw, haw! And you didn't know Dirk Stogpens was a privateer? a—what people call a pirate? a sea-robber?"

"Oh, Dirk! Dirk! How you have deceived me! But wait till you come home!"

"He will never come home. Prepare yourself, madam, for evil news. He was killed in the attack on the brig. Ah, we all lamented him. Yes, you may weep; yet consider how much wiser it was of him to meet his end battling stoutly than to come to it at the end of a halter, as I am like to do unless you shelter me. For your husband's sake, I ask you to hide me for a few days. I am Captain Kidd."

Though the widow had been drowned in tears a

moment before, at the mention of that dread name she nearly dropped from fright. "Spare me! Spare me!" she cried, going on her knees and lifting her hands in appeal.

"Why, ma'am," replied Kidd, in real surprise, "I'm not going to hurt anybody. Do you think so ill of me as that? Well, I have been a hard man, no doubt, but I'm not for pirating in fresh-water towns like Albany. Dirk has been dead these eighteen months, so it's no use mourning for him now. And see: here's a purse of his earnings in our company. Don't refuse it ma'am, for there's solid yellow comfort in it."

The Widow Stogpens was sooner consoled that one might have thought, and though she took the relic with lamentations, she took it nevertheless, and after a dutiful parley and protest consented to keep the captain in her spare room in the garret till the search that was a-making for him should be over. He kept close for several days, receiving his meals from the widow and carefully chewing them on the right side of his mouth, for on the left side was the hollow—rather tender—in which he wore the golden tooth the Devil had given to him when he burned his Bible. "A golden tooth?" inquired the relic, in one of the long conversations whereby he tried to modify the dreariness of his seclusion.

"Yes, it gives me the power to turn anything to gold that I bite upon. I don't know how long the gift will last, so I've

been nibbling a quantity of copper money and tin cups, and my men buried them the other night over at Coeymans, on Beeren Island, and at the place they've already named the Kidden hooghten, near the mouth of Norman's Kill. So, now, if you've any such matter as a couple of andirons or a few dishes you'd like me to change for you, in the way of pay for my lodging, bring them in."

And he was as good as his word. Confounded with the possession of so much wealth, the widow turned several of her plates into crowns and squandered them royally on new petticoats, shoes, buckles, combs, fans, girdles, and lace, to the joyous astonishment of the shopkeepers and the mystification of her neighbors. Such a change from the prudence of her ways could not fail to arouse comment, and Captain Kidd began presently to be alarmed at the frequency of calls in the rooms below, and to suffer greatly at having to contain all the profanity that at other times had free vent. The Devil's gift was removable, and as Kidd was in the habit of smoking a short pipe, the tooth would become unendurably hot after a dozen pulls, so that he was fain to yank it out and put it on a chest of drawers to cool. Leaving it there one evening he sauntered down to the sitting room for a glass of Hollands and a toast of his shins at the fire, when there came a lively rapping at the door and a scuffle of feet on the walk. Suspecting that he had

been traced to the house and was wanted, Kidd flung up a back window, leaped out upon the turf, and was gone from Albany forever. How the widow explained matters, if it really was a search party,—for it may have been a church committee to protest against Dame Stogpen's extravagance,—Kidd never knew; at least he never inquired; and the next that was heard of him was that he was hanged.

On the morning after his abrupt disappearance Goedevrouw Stogpens awoke with an odd feeling in her mouth, and grinning seriously at herself in the glass she discovered the Devil's tooth stoutly lodged in a hollow of her jaw. She bounced out of bed in a trice, picked up her battered pewter snuff-box and bit upon it. She cried aloud for joy, for the snuff-box was of gold. For several minutes she employed herself with gnawing and gnashing at various small belongings, and was in a way to become the rival in riches of the Rensselaers and Duyckincks and the other patroons down the river before breakfast; but a thought came to her that made her leave biting of her tableware and caused her to plump her chair so vehemently that the breath was knocked out of her for several seconds: the tooth was not movable; it was lodged fast. How, then, was she to eat? She bit on a crust and it became as stone. It was gold. By cautiously stowing her food well over to the right side of her mouth she managed to get

enough to stay the cravings of appetite, and fortified likewise with a draught of Hollands, which the tooth had no power to solidify, she went straight to Petrus Huysmans, the blacksmith, who, for a consideration, would extract an aching tooth and give his patient full money's worth in time and pains; and he hauled out the offending member.

There is no doubt that the Devil put that tooth in Vrouw Stogpen's jaw in pure kindness of spirit, with which we know him to be occasionally overcome, and as pay for the good will she had shown to Captain Kidd, his pet and pupil. But never accept the Devil's gifts. They always bring bad luck. True, they may be forced upon you, as they were on Vrouw Stogpens, and in such a case a priest and a surgeon may be needed to help you free. The widow neglected the parson. Result: the blacksmith gossiped about her new tooth—a tooth that dented under his turnkey like metal; that was yellow, like gold; that left yellow streaks on the instrument; and other gossips, taking up the story and adorned it until they had made out the unhappy woman to be a witch, and vowed they had seen her riding above the roofs on a broomstick on nights when the weather was thick. Some affected that she had bought the tooth to replace one she had lost by walking into her bedpost after putting out the candle, and one or two discoursed of a new way of filling hollow teeth with metal; but

these affected the prevailing belief not a whit, and, watched, worried, and maligned, Vrouw Stogpens allowed herself to take a cold, in spite of her eight petticoats—later increased to ten—and so perished. As for the tooth, it is believed that she cast it into the fire, and that as it melted it gave off blue flames that danced up the chimney in the shape of little imps.

THE ONANDAGA FAIRIES
CHARLES M. SKINNER

The Onondagas are a dull, peaceful, farming people who occupy a reservation of six thousand fertile acres in central New York. Their pristine wildness has disappeared, they are noted for honesty and do not beat their children. While missionaries have striven with them and induced a nominal acceptance of Christianity, they continue some of their pagan dances and ceremonies, and little is one to make them better workmen. Hiawatha, or Hoyawentha, greatest of Indians, they claim as their tribesman, and say that he was born near the end of the sixteenth century. Among the old faiths that have survived the chapel and the school is a belief in fairies: little people who abounded near Palatine Bridge, and

were known as "stone throwers," in spite of their kindly disposition. Men now living seriously declare that they have seen them, and that they could appear and vanish at pleasure.

A hunter who lived in the seventeenth century enjoyed the good will of these elves and for no reason save that his ill-luck aroused their compassion. He had been absent on the chase for some days, but nothing had fallen beneath his hand. Tired and discouraged, he sank down in the wood to rest; but becoming aware of a presence, he looked up and saw a very small woman standing beside him. She bade him be cheered, for he should find gold and silver, such as the white traders likes, and should kill as many animals as he pleased; that he had but to call them and they would offer themselves to his knife. He seems to have neglected the gold and silver, but he always had his dinner when he wanted it, after that meeting.

In later times a feeble old woman, while walking with her grandchild, met one of the fairies, who commiserated with her upon her rheumatism and her bent back, and told her to order the child to walk on, that he might not see the gift she would confer upon her. After the boy had passed some rods along the road the fairy handed a comb to the beldam and bade her use it. The old woman did so, and noticed at each passage of the implement through her grizzled locks that the hair was growing darker and darker. She felt of her face and

broke into a joyous laugh, for the wrinkles were leaving her brow and her skin was becoming softer smoother; she was growing young. Had she kept silence the transformation would, in a few minutes, have been complete, for it appears needful that supernatural gifts shall not be questioned or too closely noticed. But at the sound of her laugh the child, who was running among the trees in advance, stopped and looked back. This broke the spell. With a wailing cry, "Dear child, you have destroyed me!" the woman fell dead.

How the Black Horse Was Beaten

Charles M. Skinner

Sam Hart, of Woburn, was well known in the Bay State in the later years of the eighteenth century, for he was a lover of swift horses, a fearless rider, a layer of shocking wagers, and a regular attendant at fairs, races, and other manner of doubtful enterprises. He had one mare that he offered to pit against any piece of horse-flesh in the country, and he bragged about her, in season and out, making of her his chief topic of conversation and prayers, after the manner of men who drive fast horses. While taking the air on his door-step on a summer evening he was visited by a bland and dignified stranger whose closely shaven jowls, sober coat, cocked hat, and white wig made him look like a parson, but whose glittering black eyes did not agree with his

make-up. This gentleman had called to brag about his black horse, that would beat anything on legs, as he wished to prove by racing him against Hart's mare. He offered odds of three to one, with his horse into the bargain, and he would give the mare ten rods to start. The race was to begin at Central Square and the black horse must catch the mare by the tail with his teeth before Woburn Common was reached.

Sam accepted this challenge in an instant, and next morning the village emptied itself upon the street to see the fun. The word was given. There was a cry and a snap of the whip, and away went the coursers, tearing over the earth like a hurricane. The mare was supple, long-winded, and strong, yet the big black was surely gaining. His breath seemed actually to smoke, so hot was his pace. Sam began to suspect what sort of being this was behind him, and instead of ending the run in the way prescribed he made for the Baptist church. It was impossible to pull up sharply with such a headway, and the chase went three times around the building at a furious gallop before Sam could steer the mare close enough to the church door to be on holy ground. Fire sprang from the black horse's nostrils. It singed the mare's tail and the horizontally streaming coat-tails of her rider. Then the black horse went down upon his haunches, and Sam, pulling up with difficulty, dismounted. The Devil, who had been riding the black was out of his saddle first. Said he: "You have cheated one whose busi-

ness is cheating, and I'm a decent enough fellow to own up when I'm beaten. Here's your money. Catch it, for you know I can't cross holy ground, you rascal; and here's my horse; he'll be tractable enough after I've gone home, and as safe as your mare. Good luck to you."

A whiff of sulphur smoke burst up from the road and made Sam wink and cough. When he could open his eyes again the Devil was gone. He put the black horse into his stable, and had him out at all the fairs and functions, winning every race he entered. Still the neighbors doubted the blessing of the Devil, for they used to say that the black horse was still the Devil's horse, and that money won by racing—especially when it was won on a sure thing—would weigh the soul of its owner down to the warm place when he died.

Tom Dunn's Dance
on Rag Rock
Charles M. Skinner

Rag Rock, in which Wabanowi had his long sleep, was a home of sprites and demons down to the nineteenth century. Thomas Dunn knew this, and on ordinary nights he would have taken all manner of long cuts around it, for he had no fondness for things not of this world, whether they were ghosts or gospels. But on the night of his dance. having been to a husking-bee where he had "kept his spirits up by pouring spirits down," and having found so many red ears that he was in a state of high self-satisfaction, for he had kissed his pretty partner twenty times, he spunked up and chanced it straight across the hill. As he approached he saw a glow among the trees and heard a fiddle going—going like

mad. He buffeted his way through the thicket to see who of his towns-people were holding a picnic in the moonshine and dancing to such sacrilegious music; for there was dancing; he could hear the shuffle of feet. In a minute he had reached the edge of a glade lighted by torches and found there a richly dressed and merry company tripping it with such spirit as he had never seen before. He dearly liked to shake a leg in a jig or reel, and a chance like this was not to be withstood. He entered the ring, bowing and all-a-grin, and was welcomed with a shout. On a hummock of moss sat a maid without a partner, a maid whose black eyes snapped with mischief, whose lips and cheeks were rosy, and whose skirt, raised a trifle higher than common, showed a pair of marvelous neat ankles. The invitation in her smile and sidelong glance were not to be resisted. Tom caught her by the waist, dragged her to her feet, and whirled off with her into the gayest, wildest dance he had ever led. He seemed to soar above the earth. After a time he found that others had seated themselves and were watching him. This put him on his mettle, and the violin put lightening into his heels. He feated it superbly and won round on round of applause. He and the girl had separated for a matter of six feet and had set into dance each other down. As he leaped and whirled and cracked his heel in the air in an ecstasy of motion and existence Tom noticed with pain that

the freshness was leaving his partner's face, that it was becoming longer, the eyes deeper and harder. This pain deepened into dismay when he saw that the eyes had turned green and evil, the teeth had projected, sharp and yellow, below the lip, the form had grown lank and withered. He realized at last that it was the demon crew of the hill with which he was in company, and his heart grew so heavy that he could barely leap with it inside of him, yet leap he must, for he was lost unless he could keep up the dance till sunrise or unless a clergy-man should order him to stop—which was not a likely thing to happen. So he flung off his coat, hat, vest, and tie and settled into a business jog. The moon was setting. In two hours he would be free, and then—a cramp caught him in the calf, and with a roar of "God save me!" he tumbled on his back.

The cry did save him, for a witch cannot endure to hear the name of God. He saw a brief vision of scurrying forms, heard growling, hissing, and cursing in strange phrases, realized for a second that a hideous shape hung threatening over him, was blinded by a flame that stank of sulphur, then he saw and heard no more till daylight. If he was drunk, and imagined all this, how can one explain the two portraits of the witch he danced with? They were etched in fire on the handle of his jack-knife, one as she appeared when he met her, the other as she looked when his eyes were closing. A fever followed this

adventure. After he had regained his health Tom took to himself a wife, joined the church, forsook all entertainments, drank tea, and became a steady workman. He recovered his peace of mind, died a deacon, and was rewarded by having a cherub with a toothache sculptured on his gravestone.

GRINNING THE BARK OFF A TREE
DAVY CROCKETT

That Colonel Crockett could avail himself, in electioneering, of the advantages which well applied satire ensues, the following anecdote will sufficiently prove:

In the canvas of the Congressional election of 18--, Mr. ****** was the Colonel's opponent—a gentleman of the most pleasing and conciliating manners—who seldom addressed a person or a company without wearing upon his countenance a peculiarly good humoured smile. The Colonel, to counteract the influence of this winning attribute, thus alluded to it in a stump speech.

"Yes, gentlemen, he may get some votes by grinning,

for he can outgrin me—and you know that I ain't slow—and to prove to you that I am not, I will tell you an anecdote. I was concerned myself—and I was fooled a little of the wickedest. You all know I love hunting. Well, I discovered a long time ago that a 'coon couldn't stand my grin. I could bring one tumbling down from the highest tree. I never wasted powder and lead, when I wanted one of the creatures. Well, as I was walking out one night, a few hundred yards from my house, looking carelessly about me, I saw a 'coon planted upon one of the highest limbs of an old tree. The night was very moony and clear. And ol Ratler was with me, but Ratler won't bark at a 'coon—he's a queer dog in that way. So, I thought I'd bring the lark down in the usual way, by a grin. I set myself—and after grinning at the 'coon a reasonable time, found that he didn't come down. I wondered what was the reason—and I took another steady grin at him. Still, he was there. It made me a little mad; so I felt around and got an old limb about five feet long, and, planting one end upon the ground, I placed my chin upon the other, and took a rest. I then grinned my best for about five minutes; but the cursed 'coon hung on. So, finding I could not bring him down by grinning, I determined to have him—for I thought he must be a dull chap. I went over to the house, got my axe, returned to the tree, saw the 'coon still there, and began to cut away. Down it come, and I ran forward; but d____n the 'coon was there to be seen. I found that what I had taken for one,

was a large knot upon the branch of the tree and, upon looking at it closely, I saw that I had grinned all the bark off and left
the knot perfectly smooth.

"Now, fellow-citizens," continued the Colonel, "you
must be convinced that, in the grinning line, I myself am not
slow—yet, when I look upon my opponent's countenance, I
must admit that he is my superior. You must all admit it.
Therefore, be wide awake—look sharp—and do not let him
grin you out of your votes.

A Vote
for Mr. Crockett
Davy Crockett

But let us return again to the colonel—for the election is coming on, and he must run for congress. Now do not fancy, I beseech you, that since his last defeat he has been altogether idle, or that his time has been spent exclusively in hunting—for, although he has made a very considerable impression on the wild beasts, he has likewise made some impression upon the men,—for which a Kentucky boatman can vouch, who had the pleasure of meeting with him while in one of his quirky humours. This scene is best described in the colonel's own language: "I had taken old Betsy," said he, "and straggled off to the banks of the

Mississippi river; and meeting with no game, I didn't like it. I felt mighty spile if I wasn't kivured up in salt, for I hadn't had a fight in ten days; and I cum acrost a fellow floatin' down stream settin' in the stern of his boat fast asleep. Said I, "Hello, stranger! If you don't take keer your boat will run away with you—and he looked up; and said he, 'I don't value you.' ' He looked up at me slantendicler, and I looked down on him slantendicleer; and he took out a chaw of turbaccur, and said he, 'I don't value you that.' Said I, 'Cum ashore, I can whip you—I've been trying to git a fight for all the mornin';' and the varmint flapped his wings and crowed like a chicken. I ris up, shook my mane, and neighed like a horse. He run his boat plumb head foremost ashore. I stood still and sot my triggers, that is, took off my shurt, and tied my gallusses tight round my waist—and at it we went. He was a right smart koon, but hardly a bait for such a fellur as me. I put it to him mighty droll. In ten minutes he yelled enough, and swore I was a ripstavur. Said I, 'Ain't I the yaller flower of the forest? And I am all brimstone but the head and ears, and that's aquafortis.' Said he, 'Stranger, you are a beauty: and if I know'd your name I'd vote for you next election.' Said I, 'I'm that same David Crockett. You know what I'm made of. I've got the closest shootin' rifle, the best 'coon dog, the biggest ticlur, and the ruffest rackin-horse in the district. I can kill more lickur, fool more varmints,

and cool out more men than any man you can find in all Kentucky.' Said he, 'Good mornin', stranger—I'm satisfied.' Said I, "Good mornin', sir; I feel much better since our meetin';' but after I got away a piece, I said, 'Hello, friend, don't forget that vote.' "

BACKWOODS AMUSEMENTS

DAVY CROCKETT

"**A**fter the dinner was over," said the colonel, "I, with the remainder of the company, retired to the famous 'East Room.' I had drank a glass or two of wine, and felt in a right good humour, and was walking about gazing at the furniture, and at the splendid company with which it was filled. I noticed that many persons observed me; and just at that time, a young gentleman stepped up to me and said, "I presume, sir, you are from the backwoods?"

"Yes, sir."

"A friend whispering to me at the time, said it was the president's son; and as I had never been introduced to him, I

know'd he wanted to have some fun at my expense, because after I spoke the first word, you might have heard a pin drop. All was silence. So I thought I would keep it up. Mr. A then asked me, 'What were the amusements in the backwoods.' "Oh," said I, "fun alive there. Our people are all divided into classes, and each class has a particular sort of fun; so a man is never at a loss, because he knows which class he belongs to."

"How is that?" said Mr. A.

"We have four classes," said I, "in the backwoods. The first class have a table with some green truck on it, and its got pockets; and they knock a ball about on it to get it into the pockets," (billiard table) "and they see a mighty heap of fun. They are called the quality of our country, but to that class I don't belong."

"Then there is the second class," said I. "They take their rifles and go out about sunrise, and put up a board with a black spot on it, about a hundred yards off, and they shoot from morning till night for anything you please. They see a mighty heap of fun too; and I tell you what, I am mighty hard to beat as a second rate hand in that class."

"The third class," said I, "is composed of our little boys. They go out about light with their bows and arrows, and put up a leaf against a tree, and shoot from morning till night for persimmons, or whortleberries, or some such thing; and they see a mighty heap of fun too."

But the fourth class," said I, "oh, bless me! They have fun. This is composed of the women, and all who choose to join them. When they want a frolic, they just go into the woods and scrape away the leaves, and sprinkle the ground with corn bran, and build some large light wood fires round about, raise a banjo, and begin to dance. May be, you think they don't go to their death upon a jig, but they do, for I have frequently gone there the next morning, and raked up my two hands full of toe nails."

"By this time," says the colonel, "I have finished giving an account of our amusements, the whole house was convulsed with laughter, and I slipped off and went to my lodgings."

I asked him, what prompted him to tell the above story?

He said, that "most persons believed every thing which was said about the backwoods, and he thought he would tell a good story while he was at it. Besides," said he, "the object in questioning me at such a place was to confuse me, and laugh at my simplicity, and I thought I would humour the thing."

THE CHALLENGE
DAVY CROCKETT

During the colonel's first winter in Washington, a caravan of wild animals was brought to the city and exhibited. Large crowds attended the exhibition; and prompted by common curiosity, one evening Colonel Crockett attended. "I had just got in," said he; "the house was very much crowded, and the first thing I noticed was two wild cats in a cage. Some acquaintance asked me 'if they were like the wild cats in the backwoods?' and I was looking at them, when one turned over and died. The keeper ran up and threw some water on it. Said I, "Stranger, you are wasting your time. My looks kills them things; and you had better hire me to go out here, or I will kill every varmint you've got in your caravan.' While I and he were talking, the lions began to roar. Said I, "I

won't trouble the American lion, because he is some kin to me, but turn out the English lion—turn him out—turn him out—I can whip him for a ten dollar bill, and the zebra may kick occasionally during the fight.' This created some fun; and I then went to another part of the room, where a monkey was riding a pony. I was looking on and some member said to me, 'Crockett, don't that monkey favour General Jackson?' 'no,' said I, 'but I'll tell you who it does favour. It looks like one of your boarders, Mr. ——, of Ohio' There was a loud burst of laughter at my saying so; and upon turning round, I saw Mr. ——, of Ohio, within about three feet of me. I was in a right awkward fix; but I bowed to the company, and told 'em, 'I had either slandered the monkey, or Mr.—— of Ohio, and if they would tell me which, I would beg his pardon.' The thing passed off; and next morning, as I was walking the pavement before my door, a member came up to me, and said, 'Crockett, Mr. ——, of Ohio, is going to challenge you.' Said I, 'Well, tell him I am a fighting fowl. I 'spose if I am challenged I have the right to choose my weapon?' 'Oh, yes,' said he, 'Then tell him,' said I, 'that I will fight him with bows and arrows.'

How Bill Stout Settled a Mortgage

Charles M. Skinner

Thirteen miles from Russellville, Kentucky, lived the Widow King, on a tract of three hundred acres her husband had left to her. He also left a mortgage, and although the amount unpaid was less than four hundred dollars, the widow's creditor was troublesome. Unversed in business affairs, and hoping for a good crop that would enable her to clear away all indebtedness, she had recourse to a notorious skinflint of Logan County, who protested an interest in her and her orphans, and provided her with the sum she wished—at sixty percent a year, compound interest. The crop that year was but ordinary, so the widow sold a slave and a horse. Next year it was ordinary, too, so she parted with her other slaves

and gave up furniture, dishes, glass, and farming tools, retaining only material enough for housekeeping' but even this did not suffice, and the usurer posted a foreclosure notice on her gate. Of course the rascal had the law on his side, but there were parts of the land in the first half century of our history where the public opinion that made law was higher than the law it made. Such was the faith of Major Bill Stout, who, having served for several terms as sheriff, had resolved himself into a committee for the administration of justice, if not of law, and who inspired a wholesome respect for himself and for right conduct in the breasts of the unruly. Several outrages, murders, and robberies were punished by him, for he was an excellent shot, and his right thus to act as judge, jury, and executioner appears never to have been questioned by his fellow citizens, who, indeed were grateful to him for the saving of expense and bother.

The usurer who had possessed himself of most of the Widow King's effects, and who was now in a fine way to get her farm, was walking through his corn-patch on a sunny afternoon, wondering if a benign Providence would so shape events that he would one day hold a mortgage on every house in Russellville and be able to raise his interest charges to seventy-five percent, when he came to an abrupt stop, for he found a cocked rifle at his breast and at the other end of this weapon stood Bill Stout, looking particularly grim. In a great

trembling the rascal cried: "What is the matter, Major? Why do you point that gun at me? What have I done?"

"Oh, nothing to me, Harris, but Old Master" (here the major glanced reverently aloft) "has sent me to kill you and throw you into that hole. He says that you are not fit to live among men."

"Oh, Major Stout, have mercy! Be good! Have mercy!"

"Don't pray to me. I have nothing to do with it. Pray to Old Master. He may help you. I can't."

O, Lord, save my life. O, Lord, be good to my wife and children."

"Ah, that's good. Now, while you're at it, put in a word for the widow and orphans you have ruined."

"Yes—yes; have mercy on me, and on Mrs. King, and the King brats, and me, and—"

"Hold on, now. Pray for each one of the King family, by name."

"Yes, I'll do anything for them, and for you, if you'll only spare me."

"Oh, you've decided on that, eh? Very well; I may— mind, I don't promise, but I may—let you off if you give back her belongings and release her mortgage."

"Oh! O-o-oh, my money! My money! To think of being robbed of my hard-earned money, like this! O-oh!"

The major raised his gun.

"Hold on! Hold on! I'll do it!"

Stout had come prepared. The needful papers, together with a quill and a vial of ink, were in his pocket. He placed these on a smooth log and Harris recorded his promise in steadfast black and white, though the tears started and his heart-strings tugged when he wrote the introduction: "Of my own free will and consent, I hereby," and so forth.

Major Stout resumed: "Now, I'll let you go, perhaps, on two conditions.

One is that you meet me at nine o'clock tomorrow morning at the clerk's office in Russellville and acknowledge the release. If you fail in that I'll chase you, if it's from Lake Superior to the Gulf of Mexico, and kill you on sight. The other is that you shall not mention my part in this affair to anybody. You have no witnesses, for that matter, but if this meeting were known the widow might refuse to take back her property. Understand?"

"I understand."

The major watched Mr. Harris as he went homeward, clutching at his hair and beating his breast. Then he looked at his rifle, whistled down its barrel, and departed. Next morning the Widow King came into her own again, Major Stout looked large and happy, and Mr. Harris, albeit aged and worn, experienced a new sensation, for the clergyman spoke to him pleasantly and the townsfolk lifted their hats and shook his hand.

THE NOTORIOUS JUMPING FROG
OF CALAVERAS COUNTY
MARK TWAIN

In compliance with the request of a friend of mine, who wrote me from the East, I called on good-natured, garrulous old Simon Wheeler, and inquired after my friend's friend, Leonidas W. Smiley, as requested to do, and I hereunto append the result. I have a lurking suspicion that Leonidas W. Smiley is a myth; that my friend never knew such a personage; and that he only conjectured that if I asked old Wheeler about him, it would remind him of his infamous Jim Smiley, and he would go to work and bore me to death with some exasperating reminiscence of him as long and as tedious as it should be useless to me. If that was the design, it succeeded.

I found Simon Wheeler dozing comfortably by the bar-room stove of the dilapidated tavern in the decayed mining camp of Angel's, and I noticed that he was fat and bald-headed, and had an expression of winning gentleness and simplicity upon his tranquil countenance. He roused up, and gave me good-day. I told him a friend of mine had commissioned me to make some inquiries about a cherished companion of his boyhood named Leonidas W. Smiley, a young minister of the Gospel, who he had heard was at one time a resident of Angel's Camp. I added that if Mr. Wheeler could tell me anything about this Reverend Leonidas W. Smiley, I would feel under many obligations to him.

Simon Wheeler backed me into a corner and blockaded me there with his chair, and then sat down and reeled off the monstrous narrative which follows this paragraph. He never smiled, he never frowned, he never changed his voice from the gentle-flowing key to which he tuned his initial sentence, he never betrayed the slightest suspicion of enthusiasm; but all through the interminable narrative there ran a vein of impressive earnestness and sincerity which showed me plainly that, so far from his imagining that there was anything ridiculous or funny about his story, he regarded it as a really important matter, and admired its two heroes as men of transcendent genius in finesse. I let him go on in his own way, and never interrupted him once.

"Rev. Leonidas W. H'm, Reverend Le—well, there was a feller here once by the name of Jim Smiley, in the winter of '49—or may be it was the spring of '50— I don't recollect exactly, somehow, though what makes me think it was one or the other is because I remember the big flume warn't finished when he first come to the camp; but any way, he was the curiosest man about always betting on anything that turned up you ever see, if he could get anybody to bet on the other side; and if he couldn't he'd change sides. Any way that suited the other man would suit him—any way just so's he got a bet, he was satisfied. But still he was lucky, uncommon lucky; he most always come out winner. He was always ready and laying for a chance; there couldn't be no solit'ry thing mentioned but that feller e'd offer to bet on it, and take any side you please, as I was just telling you. if there was a horse-race, you'd find him flush or you'd find him busted at the end of it; if there was a dog fight, he'd bet on it; if there was a cat fight, he'd bet on it; if there was a chicken fight, he'd bet on it; if there was two birds setting on a fence, he would bet you on which one would fly first; or if there was a camp-meeting, he would be there reg'lar to bet on Parson Walker, which he judged to be the best exhorter about here, and so he was too, and a good man. If he even see a straddle-bug start to go any-where, he would bet you how long it would take him to get to—to wherever he was going to, and if you took him up, he

would foller that straddle-bug to Mexico but what he would find out where he was bound for and how long he was on the road. Lots of the boys here has seen that Smiley, and can tell you about him. Why it never made no difference to him—he'd bet on any thing—the dangdest feller. Parson Walker's wife laid very sick once, for a good while, and it seemed as if they warn't going to save her; but one morning he come in, and Smiley up and asked him how she was, and he said she was considable better—thank the Lord for his inf'nite mercy—and coming on so smart that with the blessing of Prov'dence she'd get well yet; and Smiley, before he thought says, "Well I'll resk two-and-a-half she don't anyway."

  "Thish-yer Smiley had a mare—the boys called her the fifteen minute nag, but that was only in fun, you know, because of course she was faster than that—and he used to win money on that horse, for all she was so slow and always had the asthma, or the distemper, or the consumption, or something of that kind. They used to give her two or three hundred yards start, and then pass her under way; but always at the fag end of the race she'd get excited and desperate-like, and come cavorting and straddling up, and scattering her legs around limber, sometimes in the air, and sometimes out to one side among the fences, and kicking up m-o-r-e dust and raising m-o-r-e racket with her coughing and sneezing and blowing her nose—and always fetch up at the stand just about

a neck ahead, as near as you could cipher it down.

"And he had a little small bull-pup, that to look at him you'd think he warn't worth a cent but to set around and look ornery and lay for a chance to steal something. But as soon as money was up on him he was a different dog; his under-jaw'd begin to stick out like the fo'castle of a steamboat, and his teeth would uncover and shine like the furnaces. And a dog might tackle him and bully-rag him, and bite him, and throw him over his shoulder two or three times, and Andrew Jackson—which was the name of the pup—Andrew Jackson would never let on but what he was satisfied, and hadn't expected nothing else—and the bets being doubled and doubled on the other side all the time, till the money was all up; and then all of a sudden he would grab that other dog jest by the j'nt of his hind leg and freeze to it—not chaw, you understand, but only just grip and hang on till they throwed up the sponge, if it was a year. Smiley always come out winner on that pup, till he harvested a dog once that didn't have no hind legs, because they'd been sawed off in a circular saw, and when the thing had gone along far enough, and the money was all up, and he come to make a snatch for his pet holt, he see in a minute how he's been imposed on, and how the other dog had him in the door, so to speak, and he 'peared surprised, and then he looked sorter discouraged-like, and didn't try no more to win the fight, and so he got shucked out bad.

He gave Smiley a look, as much to say his heart was broke, and it was his fault for putting up a dog that hadn't no hind legs for him to take holt of, which was his main dependence in a fight, and then he limped off a piece and laid down and died. It was a good pup, was that Andrew Jackson, and would have made a name for hisself if he'd lived, for the stuff was in him and he had genius—I know it, because he hadn't no opportunities to speak of, and it don't stand to reason that a dog could make such a fight as he could under them circumstances if he hadn't no talent. It always makes me feel sorry when I think of that last fight of his, and the way it turned out."

Well, thish-yer Smiley had rat-tarriers, and chicken cocks, and tomcats and all them kind of things, till you couldn't rest, and you couldn't fetch nothing for him to bet on but he'd match you. He ketched a frog one day, and took him home and said he cal'lated to educate him; and so he never done nothing for three months but set in his back yard and learn that frog to jump. And you bet you, he did learn him, too. He'd give him a little punch behind, and the next minute you'd see that frog whirling in the air like a doughnut—see him turn one summerset, or may be a couple, if he got a good start, and come down flat-footed and all right, like a cat. He got him up so in the matter of ketching flies, and kep' him in practice so constant that he'd nail a fly every time as fur as he could see him. Smiley said all a frog wanted was education, and he

could do 'most anything—and I believe him. Why I've seen
him set Dan'l Webster down here on this floor—Dan'l Webster
was the name of the frog—and sing out "Flies, Dan'l, flies!"
and quicker'n you could wink he'd spring straight up and
snake a fly off'n the counter there and flop down on the floor
ag'in as solid as a gob of mud, and fall to scratching the side of
his head with his hind foot as indifferent as if he hadn't no idea
he'd been doin' any more'n any frog might do. You never see a
frog so modest and straightfor'ard as he was, for all he was so
gifted. And when it come to fair and square jumping on a dead
level, he could get over more ground at one straddle than any
animal of his breed that you ever see. Jumping on a dead level
was his strong suit, you understand, and when it came to that,
Smiley would ante up money on him as long as he had a red.
Smiley was monstrous proud of his frog, and well he might be,
for fellers that had traveled and been everywhere all said he
laid over any frog that ever they see.

"Well, Smiley kep' the beast in a little lattice box, and
he used to fetch him down town sometimes and lay for a bet.
One day a feller—a stranger in the camp, he was—come acrost
him with his box, and says:

"What might it be that you've got in the box?"

"And Smiley says, sorter indifferent-like, 'It might be a
parrot, or it might be a canary, maybe, but it ain't—it's only just
a frog.'

"And the feller took it, and looked at it careful, and turned it round this way and that, and says, 'H'm—so 'tis. Well, what's *he* good for?'

" 'Well,' Smiley says, easy and careless, 'he's good enough for one thing, I should judge—he can outjump any frog in Calaveras county.'

"The feller took the box again, and took another long, particular look, and gave it back to Smiley, and says, very deliberate, 'Well,' he says, 'I don't see no p'ints about that frog that's any better'n any other frog.'

" 'Maybe you don't,' Smiley says. 'Maybe you understand frogs and maybe you don't understand 'em; maybe you've had experience, and maybe you ain't only an amature, as it were. Anyways, I've got my opinion and I'll resk forty dollars that he can outjump any frog in Calaveras county.'

"And the feller studied a minute, and then says, kinder sad like, 'Well, I'm only a stranger here, and I ain't got no frog, but if I had a frog, I'd bet you.'

"And then Smiley says, 'that's all right—that's all right—if you'll hold my box a minute, I'll go and get you a frog.' And so the feller took the box, and put up his forty dollars along with Smiley's, and set down to wait.

"So he set there a good while thinking and thinking to hisself, and then he got the frog out and prized his mouth open and took a teaspoon and filled him full of quail shot—

and filled him pretty near up to his chin—and set him on the floor. Smiley he went to the swamp and slopped around in the mud for a long time, and finally he ketched a frog, and fetched him in, and give him to this feller, and says:

" 'Now, if you're ready, set him alongside of Dan'l, with his forepaws just even with Dan'l's, and I'll give the word.' Then he says, 'One—two—three-git!' and him and the feller touched up the frogs from behind, and the new frog hopped off lively, but Dan'l give a heave, and hysted up his shoulders— so—like a Frenchman, but it warn't no use—he couldn't budge; he was planted solid as a church, and he couldn't no more stir than if he was anchored out. Smiley was a good deal sur- prised, and he was disgusted too, but he didn't have no idea what the matter was, of course.

"The feller took the money and started away; and when he was going out at the door, he sorter jerked his thumb over his shoulder—so—at Dan'l, and says again, very deliberate, 'Well,' he says, 'I don't see no p'ints about that frog that's any better'n any other frog. '

"Smiley he stood scratching his head and looking down at Dan'l a long time, and at last he says, 'I do wonder what in the nation that frog throw'd off for—I wonder if there ain't something the matter with him—he pears to look mighty baggy, somehow.' And he ketched Dan'l by the nap of the neck, and hefted him, and says, 'Why blame my cats if he don't

weigh five pound!' and turned him upside down and he belched out a double handful of shot. And then we see how it was, and he was the maddest man—he set the frog down and took out after that feller, but he never ketched him. And—"

[Here Simon Wheeler heard his name called from the front yard, and got up to see what was wanted.] And turning to me as he moved away, he said: "Just set where you are, stranger, and rest easy—I ain't going to be gone a second."

But, by your leave, I did not think that a continuation of the history of the enterprising vagabond Jim Smiley would be likely to afford me much information concerning the Rev. Leonidas W. Smiley, and so I started away.

At the door I met the sociable Wheeler returning, and he button-holed me and recommenced:

"Well, thish-yer Smiley had a yaller one-eyed cow that didn't have no tail, only jest a short stump like a bannanner, and —"

However, lacking both time and inclination, I did not wait to hear about the afflicted cow, but took my leave.

The Glorious Whitewasher
MARK TWAIN

Saturday morning was come,
and all the summer world was bright and fresh, and brimming
with life. There was a song in every heart; and if the heart was
young the music issued at the lips. There was a cheer in every
face and a spring in every step. The locust trees were in bloom
and the fragrance of the blossoms filled the air. Cardiff Hill,
beyond the village and above it, was green with vegetation,
and it lay just far enough away to seem a Delectable Land,
dreamy, reposeful, and inviting..

Tom appeared on the sidewalk with a bucket of whitewash and a long-handled brush. He surveyed the fence, and
all gladness left him and a deep melancholy settled down
upon his spirit. Thirty yards of board fence nine feet high. Life

to him seemed hollow, and existence but a burden. Sighing he dipped his brush and passed it along the top-most plank; repeated the operation, did it again; compared the insignificant whitewashed streak with the far-reaching continent of unwhitewashed fence, and sat down on a tree-box discouraged. Jim came skipping out at the gate with a tin pail, and singing "Buffalo Gals." Bringing water from the town pump had always been hateful work in Tom's eyes before, but now it did not strike him so. He remembered that there was company at the pump. White, mulatto, and negro boys and girls were always there waiting their turns, resting, trading playthings, quarreling, fighting, skylarking. And he remembered that although the pump was only a hundred fifty yards off, Jim never got back with a bucket of water under an hour—and even then somebody generally had to go after him. Tom said:

"Say, Jim, I'll fetch the water if you whitewash some."

Jim shook his head and said:

"Can't Mars Tom. Ole missis, she tole me I got to go an git dis water an' not stop foolin' roun' wid anybody. She say she spec' Mars Tom gwine to ax me to whitewash, an' she tole me go 'long an' tend to my own business—she 'lowed *she'd* 'tend to de whitewashin'."

"Oh, never you mind what she said, Jim. That's the ways she always talks. Gimme the bucket—I won't be gone only a minute. *She* won't ever know.

"Oh, I dasn't, Mars Tom. Ole missis she'd take an' tar de head off'n me. 'Deed she would."

"*She!* She never licks anybody—whacks them over the head with her thimble—and who cares for that, I'd like to know. She talks awful, but talk don't hurt—anyways it don't if she don't cry. Jim, I'll give you a marvel I'll give you a white alley!"

Jim began to waver.

"White alley, Jim! And it's a bully taw."

"My! Dat's mighty gay marvel, *I* tell you! But Mars Tom, I's powerful 'fraid ole missis—"

"And besides, if you will I'll show you my sore toe."

Jim was only human—this attraction was too much for him. He put down his pail, took the white alley, and bent over the toe with absorbing interest while the bandage was being unwound. In another moment he was flying down the street with his pail and a tingling rear, Tom was whitewashing with vigor, and Aunt Polly was retiring from the field with a slipper in her hand and triumph in her eye.

But Tom's energy did not last. He began to think of the fun he had planned for this day, and his sorrows multiplied. Soon the free boys would come tripping along on all sorts of delicious expeditions, and they would make a world of fun of him for having to work—the very thought of it burnt him like

fire. He got out his worldly wealth and examined it—bits of toys, marbles and trash; enough to buy an exchange of work, maybe, but not half enough to buy so much as half an hour of pure freedom. So he returned his straightened means to his pocket, and gave up the idea of trying to buy the bys. At this dark and hopeless moment an inspiration burst upon him! Nothing less than a great, magnificent inspiration.

He took up his brush and went tranquilly to work. Ben Rogers hove in sight presently—the very boy, of all boys, whose ridicule he had been dreading. Ben's gait was the hop-skip-and-jump—proof enough that his heart was light and his anticipations high. He was eating an apple, and giving a long, melodious whoop, at intervals, followed by a deep-toned ding-dong-dong, ding-dong-dong, for he was personating a steamboat. As he drew near, he slackened speed, took the middle of the street, leaned far over to starboard and rounded too ponderously andwith laborious pomp and circumstance—for he was personating the Big Missouri, and considered himself to be drawing nine feet of water. He was boat and captain and engine-bells combined, so he had to imagine himself standing on his own hurricane-deck giving the orders and executing them:

"Stop her, sir! Ting-a-ling-ling." The headway ran almost out and he drew up slowly toward the sidewalk.

"Ship up to back! Ting-ling-ling!" His arms straightened and stiffened down his sides.

"Set her back on the stabboard! Ting-a-ling-ling! Chow! ch-chow-wow!" The left hand began to transcribe circles.

"Stop the stabboard! Ting-a-ling-ling! Stop the labboard! Come ahead on the stabboard side! Stop her! Let you r outside turn over slow! Ting-a-ling-ling! Chow-ow-ow! Get out that head line! Lively now! Come—out with your springline—what're you about there! Take a turn round that stump with the bight of it! Stand by that stage, now—let her go! Done with the engines, sir! Ting-a-ling-ling! *Sh't s'h't! sh't*" (trying the gaugecocks).

Tom went on whitewashing—paid no attention to the streamboat. Ben stared a moment and then said:

"Hi-yi! You're up a stump, ain't you!"

No answer. Tom surveyed his last touch with the eye of an artist, then he gave his brush another gentle sweep and surveyed the result, as before. Ben ranged up alongside of him. Tom's mouth watered for the apple, but he stuck to his work. Ben said:

"Hello, old chap, you got to work, hey?"

Tom wheeled suddenly and said:

"Why, it's you, Ben! I warn't noticing."

"Say—I'm going in a-swimming, I am. Don't you wish

you could? But of course you'd druther work—wouldn't you? Course you would!"

Tom contemplated the boy a bit, and said:

"What do you call work?"

"Why ain't *that* work?"

Tom resumed his whitewashing, and answered carelessly:

"Well, maybe it is, and maybe it ain't. All I know is, it suits Tom Sawyer."

"Oh, come now, you don't mean to let on that you like it?"

The brush continued to move.

"Like it? Well, I don't see why I oughn't to like it. Does a boy get a chance to whitewash a fence every day?"

That put the thing in a new light. Ben stopped nibbling his apple. Tom swept his brush daintily back and forth — stepped back to note the effect—added a touch here and there—criticized the effect again—Ben watching every move and getting more and more interested, more and more absorbed. Presently he said:

"Say, Tom, let *me* whitewash a little."

Tom considered, was about to consent; but he altered his mind:

"No—no—I reckon it wouldn't hardly do, Ben. You see,

Aunt Polly's awful particular about this fence—right here on the street, you know—but if it was the back fence I wouldn't mind and she wouldn't. Yes, she's awful particular about this fence; it's got to be done very careful; I reckon there ain't one boy in a thousand, maybe two thousand, that can do it the way it's got to be done."

"No—is that so? Oh, come on, now—lemme just try. Only just a little—I'd let *you*, if you was me, Tom."

"Ben, I'd like to, honest injun; but Aunt Polly—well, Jim wanted to do it, but she wouldn't let him; Sid wanted to and she wouldn't let Sid. Now don't you see how I'm fixed? If you was to tackle this fence and anything was to happen to it—"

"Oh, shucks, I'll be just as careful. Now lemme try. Say—I'll give you the core of my apple."

"Well, here—No, Ben, now don't. I'm afeared—"

"Ill give you *all* of it!"

Tom gave up the brush with reluctance in his face, but alacrity in his heart. And while the late steamer *Big Missouri* worked and sweated in the sun, the retired artist sat on a barrel in the shade close by, dangled his legs, munched his apple, and planned the slaughter of more innocents. There was no lack of material; boys happened along very little while; they came to jeer, but remained to whitewash. By the time Ben was fagged out, Tom had traded the next chance to Billy Fisher for

a kite, in good repair; and when he played out, Johnny Miller bought in for a dead rat and a string to swing it with—and so on, and so on, hour after hour. And when the middle of the afternoon came, from being a poor, poverty-stricken boy in the morning, Tom was literally rolling in wealth. He had beside the things before mentioned, twelve marbles, part of a jew's harp, a piece of blue bottle-glass to look through, a spool cannon, a key that wouldn't unlock anything, a fragment of chalk, a glad stopper of a decanter, a tin soldier, a couple of tadpoles, six firecrackers, a kitten with only one eye, a brass door-knob, a dog-collar—but no dog—the handle of a knife, four pieces of orange-peel, and a dilapidated old window-sash.

He had a nice, good, idle time all the while—plenty of company—and the fence had three coats of whitewash on it! If he hadn't run out of whitewash, he would have bankrupted every boy in the village.

Tom said to himself that it was not such a hollow world, after all. He had discovered a great law of human action, without knowing it—namely that in order to make a man or boy covet a thing, it is only necessary to make the thing difficult to attain. If he had been a great and wise philosopher, like the writer of this book, he would now have comprehended that Work consists of whatever a body is *obliged* to do, and that Play consists of whatever a body is

not obliged to do. And this would help him to understand why constructing artificial flowers or performing on a treadmill is work, while rolling tenpins or climbing Mont Blanc is only amusement. There are wealthy gentlemen in England who drive four-horse passenger-coaches twenty or thirty miles on a daily line, in the summer, because the privilege costs them considerable money; but if they were offered wages for the service, that would turn it into work and then they would resign.

The boy mused awhile over the substantial change which had taken place in his worldly circumstances, and then wended toward headquarters to report.

How Mr. Rabbit
Was Too Sharp for Mr. Fox
Joel Chandler Harris

"**U**ncle Remus,' said the little boy one evening, when he had found the old man with little or nothing to do, "did the fox kill and eat the rabbit when he caught him with the Tar-Baby?"

"Law, honey, ain't I tell you 'bout dat?" replied the old darkey, chuckling slyly. "I 'clar ter grashus I ought er tole you dat, but old man Nod was ridin' on my eyeleds 'twel a leetle mo'n I'd a dis'-member'd my own name, en den on top dat here come yo' mammy hollerin after you.

"W'at I tell you w'en I fus begin? I tole you Brer Rabbit wuz a monstus soon creetur; leas'ways dats's w'at I laid out fer ter tell you. Well, den, honey, don't you go en make no

udder calkalashuns, kaze in dem days Brer Rabbit en his fambly wuz at de head er de gang w'en enny racket wuz on han', an dar day stayed. Fo' uou begins fer ter wipe yo' eyes 'bout Brer Rabbit, you wait en see whar'bouts Brer Rabbit gwineter fetch up at. But dat's needer yer ner dar.

"W'en Brer Fox fine Brer Rabbit mixt up wid de Tar Baby, he feel mighty good, en he roll on de groun' en laff. Bimeby he up'n say, sezee:

"Well, I speck I got you dis time, Brer Rabbit,' sezee" "maybe I ain't, but I Speck I is. You been runnin' round here sassin' atter me a mighty long time, but I speck you done come ter de een' er de row. You bin cuttin' up yo' capers en bouncin' roun' in dis neighborhood ontwel you come ter b'leeve you'sef de boss er de whole gang. En den youer allers some'rs whar you got no bizness,' sez Brer Fox, sezee. 'Who ax you fer ter come en strike up a'quaintance wid dish yer Tar-Baby? En who stuck you up dar whar you iz? Nobody in de roun worril. You des tuck and jam you'sef on dat Tar-Baby widout waitin fer enny invite,' sez Brer Fox, sezee, 'en dar you is, en dar you'll stay twel I fixes up a bresh-pile and fires her up, kaze I'm gwineter bobbycue you dis day, sho' sez Brer Fox, sezee.

'Den Brer Rabbit talk mighty 'umble.

"I don't keer w'at you do wid me, Brer Fox,' sezee, 'so

you don't fling me in dat brier-patch. Roas' me, Brer Fox,' sezee, 'but don't fling me in dat brier-patch,' sezee.

"Hit's so much trouble fer ter kindle a fier,' sez Brer Fox, sezee, 'dat I speck I'll hatter hang you,' sezee.

"Hang me des ez high as you please, Brer Fox,' sez Brer rabbit, sezee, 'but do fer de Lord's sake don't fling me in dat brier-patch,' sezee.

"I anin't got no string,' sez brer Fox, sezee, 'en now I speck I'll hatter drown you, sezee.'

"Drown me des ez deep ez you please, Brer Fox,' sez Brer rabbir, sezee, 'but don't fling me in dat brier-patch, sezee.

"Dey ain't no water nigh,' sez Brer Fox, sezee, 'en now I speck I'll hatter skin you,' sezee.

"Skin me, Brer Fox,' sez Brer rabbit, sezee, 'snatch out my eyeballs, t'ar out my years by de roots, en cut off my legs,' sez Brer rabbit, sezee, 'but do please, Brer Fox, don' fling me in dat brier-patch,' sezee.

"Co'se Brer Fox wanter hurt Brer Rabbit bad ez he kin, so he cotch 'im by de behime legs an slung 'im right in der middle er de brier-patch. Dar wuz considerbul flutter whar Brer Rabbit struck de bushes, en Brer fox sorter hangin roun' fer ter see a'at wuz gwineter happen. Bimeby he hear somebody call 'im, en way up de hill he see Brer Rabbit settin' cross-legged on a chikapin log koamin' de pitch outen his har

wid a chip. Den Brer Fox know dat he bin swop off mighty bad. Brer Rabbit wuz bleedzed fer ter fling back some er his sass, en he holler out:

"Bred and bawn in a brier-patch, Brer Fox—bred and bawn in a brier-patch!' en wid dat he skip out des ez lively ez a cricket in de embers."

Where the Harrycane Comes From
Joel Chandler Harris

While Uncle Remus was telling the little boy how the negro man had been frightened by his master, the clouds began to gather in the southwest, dark and-threatening. They ro0se higher and higher, and presently they began to fly swiftly overhead. Uncle Remus studied them carefully for a moment, and then remarked sententiously:—

"Mo'win' dan water, I speck."

"How can you tell, Uncle Remus?" asked the little boy.

"Caze when cloud got water in it you kin see de shadder er de rain; you can see where she starts ter break off fum de cloud. Dat cloud yonder look black, but she's all stirred up; you can't see no rain trailin' down. She look like she been tousled and tumbled."

Just then the old man and the little boy felt the cool wind strike their faces, and the leaves of the trees began to rustle. Straightway they heard a sighing sound in the distance, which gradually increased to a steady roar, accompanied by an occasional gleam of lightening and rumbling of thunder.

"I speck we better git in under de shingles," said Uncle Remus. "It mought be a harrycane, and den agin it mought n't."

They went into the old negro's cabin, and sat there watching the approaching storm. It was not much of a storm after all. There was a very high wind, which seemed to blow through the tops of the trees (as Uncle Remus expressed it, "She rid high") without reaching the ground. While the gale in the upper air was at its height, there was a sudden downpour of hail, which rattled on the roof with startling effect for a few moments. In half an hour the clouds had been whisked away out of sight, and the sun was shining again. The little boy had a good many remarks to make about the wind and the hail, and a great many questions to ask. Uncle Remus himself was unusually talkative, and, finally in response to some suggestion of the child's said:—

"Dem what done seed one harrycane ain't agwine hone atter no mo'—dat dey ain't. I use ter hear ole Miss talk 'bout a bed tick dat wuz blow'd fum Jones county mos'ter 'Gusty. Dat same harrycane blow'd de roof off'n a house whar de folks wuz eatin' supper, en did n't put de candle out. Dat

what ole Miss say," said the old man, noting the little boy's look of astonishment,—"dat what ole Miss say, an she you' gran-mammy. You kin 'spute it ef you wanter. It tuck a mule en landed 'im in de tree top, en tuck de mattress fum under a baby in de cradle en lef de baby layin' dar. I wuz stannin' right by when ole Miss sesso."

"Where do the harrycanes start from, Uncle Remus?" asked the little boy.

The old man chuckled, as he took a chew of tobacco:—

"What de use er me tellin' you, honey? You won't nigh believe me, en mo'n dat: you'll go up yander en tell Miss Sally dat de ole nigger done gone ravin' 'stracted."

"Now, Uncle Remus, you know I won't," protested the little boy.

"Well, folks lots older en bigger dan what you is ud go en do it, en not so much ez bat der eyes."

The old man paused, took off his spectacles, and rubbed his eyes with thumb and forefinger. Replacing the glasses, he looked carefully around, laid his hand confidentially on the little boy's shoulder, and said in a low whisper:—

"I'll tell you whar de harrycane starts. Dey starts in de big swamp! In a hollow tree! Down dar whar de bullace vines grows! Dat's whar dey starts."

"I don't see how that can be," said the puzzled youngster.

"I speck not," remarked Uncle Remus, dryly. "You dun-

ner how 'tis dat dat ar acorn in yo' han' is got a great big oak tree in it. Dey got ter be a startin' place. Ef trees wuz ter start out trees, you'd see a monst'us upsettin' all 'roun' ev'ey-wheres. Dey'd be trouble, mon, en a heap un it."

"But how can a harrycane start in a hollow tree, Uncle Remus?" the child asked.

"Well, suh, one time when I wuz a little bigger dan what you is, dey wuz a ole Affiky man live on de place, en he kep' a-tellin' me tales, and bimeby one day he 'low he wanter shew me some harrycane seed. I ain't had much sense, but I had 'nuff fer ter tell 'im I don't wanter look at um, kaze I fear'd dey'd sprout en come up right 'fo' my eyes. Den dat ole Affiky man, he squinch his eyes at me en tell me de tale how de har-rycane start.

"Hit's all on account er ole Sis Swamp-Owl. All de birds er de a'r sot her ole man fer ter watch de vittles one time, en he tuck'n went ter sleep en let some un steal it. Dey kotch 'im sleep, en fum dat time out dey start in ter fight 'im eve'y time he show his head in daylight. Dis make ole Sis Swamp-Owl mad, en so one day, when de hot wedder come, she make up her min' dat she gwine ter gi' de tudder birds some trouble. She come out de holler tree en sot up on de top lim's. She look to'rds sundown, rain-seeds floatin' 'roun'; she look up in de elements, dey look hazy. She tap on de tree.

"Wake up, ole man; harrycane gittin' ripe.'

"She stretch out 'er wings, so—en flop um down —dis way—en right den an dar de harrycane seed sprouted." Uncle Remus used his arms to illustrate the motion of the wings.

"When she flop 'er wings, de tree leafs 'gun ter rustle. She flop um some mo', en de lim's gun ter shake, en de win' kotch up mo' win, en git harder en harder, twel bimeby it look like it gwine ter claw de grass out de groun'. Den de thunder en de lightnin' dey jin'd it, en it des went a-whirlin'.
"Sence dat time, whenever ole Sis Owl gits tired er de crows en de jaybirds, en de bee-martins pickin' at her en her folks, she des come out en flops her wings, en dar's yo harrycane."

PAUL BUNYAN
ROBERT CAROLA

Folktales usually have a purpose, and in the case of Paul Bunyan that purpose is clear. His legend was begun in 1910 when the relatively new American lumber industry needed some creative promotion.

In 1914 W. B. Laughead of the Red River Lumber Company of Minnesota began publishing wildly exaggerated fictional articles in booklets about a giant lumberjack called Paul Bunyan. Laughead's stories and Paul Bunyan became popular when they were rewritten and republished. But the first printed stories about Paul Bunyan, written by James MacGillivray, appeared in 1910 in the *Detroit News*.

According to the tallest of tall tales about the American frontier, the giant lumberjack and logger (along with his equally gigantic blue ox named Babe), created the Grand Canyon by dragging Paul's ax behind him, the black Hills of South Dakota and Wyoming, and when Iowa and Kansas were full of mountains and the farmers couldn't plant any crops, Paul Bunyan came and flattened the land to form the Great Plains, now full of corn and wheat. He formed Mount Hood in Washington when he put out his campfire by covering it with rocks. With only four steps he could climb the Blue Mountains of Ontario, and, being the world's greatest lumberjack, he could topple ten huge trees with one swing of his ax.

And, of course, Paul Bunyan created the Mississippi River and Puget Sound just to move his logs. The story goes that Paul Bunyan had cut down many, many trees in Minnesota and had to deliver them to New Orleans. The trouble was, there was no way to move the logs. Paul decided that it would have been perfect if there was a river that ran from Minnesota to New Orleans—and so, he dug a large ditch and filled it with his dish water. And that is how the Mississippi River was born.

Babe contributed to the building of America also. Several of the lakes in Minnesota and Washington state were formed from Babe's hoof prints, and she helped Paul Bunyan straighten a road by just pulling on it. Paul Bunyan first met

babe when he was traveling in the cold northeast, where the snow was so cold it was a bright blue instead of white. When it finally stopped snowing Paul went out for a walk. On his way he saw a blue tail sticking out from the snow, and when he bent down and pulled the tail, out it came attached to a blue ox. That was Babe, who used to be white. The snow was so cold and so deep and so blue that it had turned Babe into America's only blue ox, which grew into America's biggest ox.

Some historians believe that the legend of Paul Bunyan was based on the French-Canadian logger named Fabian "Joe" Fournier, who was born in Quebec about 1845. Apparently, Fournier led the kind of adventurous life that provided fodder for camp stories, especially after he was murdered in Bay City in 1875. At one time, the reporter James MacGillivray worked as a logger for the same company as Fournier, providing interesting room for speculation about Paul Bunyan's origin.

The popularity of the Paul Bunyan stories helped generate more tall tales about other fictional heroes who helped build a new way of life for ordinary Americans. For example, Paul Bunyan was god-father to Pecos Bill, a cowboy; Joe Magarac, a steelworker, and Febold Feboldson, a prairie strongman.

Paul Bunyan, born in the American imagination soon after the twentieth century began represented strength, vitality, competence, courage, and all the other grand virtues of

American pioneers who conquered the wilderness with all its obstacles. Nothing could stop Paul Bunyan's progress across the vast country, not even giant mosquitoes or long-lasting winters that turned the wind into sheets of ice.

Poets have written of the remarkable feats of Paul Bunyan, and even an opera has been composed to celebrate Paul Bunyan, the big heart of America and its people.

Babe the Mighty Blue Ox
Glen Rounds

Babe was so strong that he could pull mighty near anything that he could be hitched to. His exact size, as I said before, is not known, for although it is said that he stood ninety-three hands high, it's not known whether that meant ordinary logger's hands, or hands the size of Paul's, which, of course, would be something else again.

However, they tell of an eagle that had been in the habit of roosting on the tip of Babe's right horn, suddenly deciding to fly to the other. Colombus Day, it was, when he started. He flew steadily, so they say, night and day, fair weather and foul, until his wing feathers were worn down to pinfeathers and a new set grew to replace them. In all, he seems

to have worn out seventeen sets of feathers on the trip, and from reaching up to brush the sweat out of his eyes so much, had worn all the feathers off the top of his head, becoming completely bald, as are all of his descendants to this day. Finally, the courageous bird won through, reaching the brass ball on the tip of the left horn on the seventeenth of March. He waved a wing weakly at the cheering lumberjacks and 'lowed as how he'd of made it sooner but for the head winds.

THE ROUND RIVER DRIVE
JAMES MACGILLIVRAY

That Round River ox-team was the biggest ever heard of, I guess. They weighed forty-eight hundred. The barn boss made them a buckskin harness from the hides of the deer we'd killed, and the bull cook used them haulin' dead timber to camp for wood supply. But that harness sure queered them oxen when it got wet. You know how buckskin will stretch?

It was rainin' one mornin' when the bull cook went for wood. He put the tongs on a big wind-fall and started for camp. The oxen pull all right, but that blame harness got stretchin', and when the bull cook gets his log into camp, it wasn't there at all.

He looks back and there was the tugs of that harness, stretched out in long lines disappearin' 'round the bend of the

road, 'most as far as he could see. He's mad and disgusted like, and he jerks the harness off and throws the tugs over a stump.

It clears up pretty soon. The sun comes out, dryin' up that harness, and when the bull cook comes out from dinner, there's his windfall hauled right into camp.

It's a fright how deep the snow gets that winter in one storm, and she'd melt just as quick.

Bunyan sent me out cruisin' one day, and if I hadn't had snowshoes I wouldn't be here to tell you. Comin' back, I hit the log road, though I wouldn't knowed it was there but for the swath line through the tree-tops. I saw a whiplash cracker lyin' there on the snow. "Hello!" says I , "someone's lost their whiplash"; and I see it as Tom Hurley's by the braid of it. I hadn't any more'n picked it up, "fore it was jerked out of my hand, and Tom yells up "Leave that whip alone, d—m ye! I've got a five hundred log peaker on the forty-foot bunks and eight horses down here, and I need the lash to get her to the landin'."

They was big trees what Bunyan lumbered that winter, and one of them pretty near made trouble.

They ust to keep a compitishin board hung in the commissary, showin' what each gang sawed for the week, and that's how it happened.

Dutch Jake and me had picked out the biggest tree we could find on the forty, and we'd put in three days on the fellin' cut with our big saw, what was three cross cuts brazed togeth-

er, makin' 80 feet of teeth. We was gettin' along fine on the fourth day when lunch time comes, and we thought we'd best get on the sunny side to eat. So we grabs our grub can and starts around that tree. We hadn't gone far when we heard a noise. Blamed if there wasn't Bill Carter and Sailor Jack sawin' at the same tree.

It looked like a fight at first, but we compromised, meetin' each other at the heart on the seventh day. They'd hacked her to fall to the north, and we'd hacked her to fall to the south, and there that blamed tree stood for a month or more, clean sawed through, but not knowin' which way to drop 'til a wind storm came along and blowed her over.

Right in front of the bunk house was a monster school-ma'am, that's two trees growed as one, so big she'd a put the linen mills out of business. Joe Benoit and Dolph Burgoyne ust to say their A,B, C's in front of her, and soon learned to swear in English. Whenever we got lost on that pyramid 40*, we'd just look around for four ways 'til we see the schoolma'am's bonnet, and then we could strike for camp around for four ways 'til we see the schoolma'am's bonnet, and then we could strike for camp.

---

*A forty-acre stand of trees

. . . She broke up early that spring. The river was run-nin' high, and black from the color of the snow, of course, and

all hands went on the drive. Bunyan was sure that we would hit either the "Sable" or Muskegon, and he cared not a dam which, fer logs was much the same allwheres.

We run that drive for four weeks, makin' about a mile a day with the rear, when we struck a camp what had been a lumberin' big and had gone ahead with its drive, what must have been almost as large as Bunyan's from the signs on the banks. They'd been cuttin' on a hill forty, too. Which was peculiar, for we didn't know there could be two such places.

We drove along for another month and hits another hill forty, deserted like the last one, and Paul begins to swear, for he sees the price of logs fallin' with all this lumberin' on the one stream.

Well, we sacked and bulled them logs for five weeks more, and blamed if we didn't strike another hill forty. Then Bunyan gets wild! "Boys," he says, "if we strike any more of them d—n camps, logs won't be worth thirty cents a thousand, and I won't be able to pay you off—perhaps some of you want to bunch her? Let's camp and talk it over," he says.

So we hits for the deserted shacks, and turnin' the pyramid corner, we who was leadin' butts right into—our schoolma'am! And there, at her feet was those two c—s what had been blown up months ago, and at their feet was the hams! Then we knowed it was Round River, and we'd druv it three times.

Did we ever locate it again? Well, some!

Tom Mellin and I runs a line west, out of Graylin', some years afterwards when logs get high, thinkin' to take them out with a dray-haul, and we finds the old camp on section thirty-seven. But the stream had gone dry, and a fire had run through that country makin' an awful slashin' and those Round River logs was charcoal.

THE SAGA OF PECOS BILL

EDWARD O'REILLY

According to the most veracious historians, Bill was born about the same time Sam Houston discovered Texas. His mother was a sturdy pioneer woman who once killed forty-five Indians with a broom-handle. He cut his teeth on a bowie knife, and his earliest playfellows were the bears and catamounts of east Texas.

When Bill was about a year old, another family moved into the country, and located about fifty miles down the river. His father decided the place was gettin' too crowded, and packed his family in a wagon and headed west.

One day after they crossed the Pecos River, Bill fell out of the wagon. As there were sixteen or seventeen other children in the family, his parents didn't miss him for four or five weeks, and then it was too late to try and find him.

That's how Bill grew up with the coyotes along the Pecos. He soon learned the coyote language, and used to hunt with them and sit on the hills and howl at night. Being so young when he got lost, he always thought he was a coyote. That's where he learned to kill deer by runnin' them to death.

One day when he was about ten years old a cow-boy came along just when Bill had matched a fight with two grizzly bears. Bill hugged the bears to death, tore off a hind leg, and was just settin' down to breakfast when this cowboy loped up and asked him what he meant by runnin' around naked that way among the varmints.

"Why, because I am a varmint," Bill told him. "I'm a coyote."

The cow-boy argued with him that he was a human, but Bill wouldn't believe him.

"Ain't I got fleas?" he insisted. "And don't I howl around all night, like a respectable coyote should do?"

"That don't prove nothin'," the cow-boy answered. "All Texans have fleas, and most of them howl. Did you ever see a coyote that didn't have a tail? Well, you ain't got no tail' so that proves you ain't a varmint."

Bill looked, and sure enough, he didn't have a tail.

"You sure got me out on a limb," says Bill. "I never noticed that before. It shows what higher education will do for a man. I believe you're right. Lead me to them humans, and I'll throw in with them."

Bill went to town with this cow-hand, and in due time he got to enjoyin' all the pleasant vices of mankind, and decided that he certainly was a human. He got to runnin' with the wild bunch, and sunk lower and lower, until he finally became a cow-boy.

It wasn't long before he was famous as a bad man. He invented the six-shooter and train-robbin' and most of the crimes popular in the old days of the West. He didn't invent cow-stealin'. That was discovered by King David in the Bible, but Bill improved on it.

There is no way of tellin' just how many men Bill did kill. Deep down he had a tender heart, however, and never killed women or children, or tourists out of season. He never scalped his victims; he was too civilized for that.

It wasn't long before Bill had killed all the bad men in west Texas, massacred all the Indians, and eat all the buffalo. So he decided to migrate to a new country where hard men still thrived and a man could pass the time away.

He saddled up his horse and hit for the West. One day he met an old trapper and told him what he was lookin' for.

"I want the hardest cow outfit in the world," he says. "Not one of these ordinary cow-stealin', Mexican-shootin' bunches of amateurs, but a real hard herd of hand-picked hellions that make murder a fine art and take some proper pride in their slaughter."

"Stranger, you're headed in the right direction,' answers the trapper. "Keep right on down this draw for a couple of hundred miles, and you'll find the very outfit. They're so hard they can kick fire out of a flint rock with their bare toes." Bill single-footed down that draw for about a hundred miles that afternoon; then he met with an accident. His horse stubbed his toe on a mountain and broke his leg, leavin' Bill afoot.

He slung his saddle over his shoulder and set off hikin' down that draw, cussin' and a-swearin'. Profanity was a gift with Bill.

All at once a big ten-foot rattlesnake quiled up in his path, set his tail to singin', and allowed he'd like to match a fight. Bill laid down his saddle and started on, carryin' the snake in his hand and spinnin' it in short loops at the Gila monsters.

About fifty miles further on, a big old mountain lion jumped off a cliff and lit spraddled out on Bill's neck. This was no ordinary lion. It weighed more than three steers and a yearlin', and was the very same lion the State of Nuovo León was

named after down in old Mexico.

Kind of chucklin' to himself, Bill laid down his saddle, and his snake and went into action. In a minute the fur was flyin' down the canyon until it darkened the sun. The way Bill knocked the animosity out of that lion was a shame. In about three minutes that lion hollered:

"I'll give up, Bill. Can't you take a joke?"

Bill let him up, and then he cinched the saddle on him and went down that canyon whoopin' and yellin', ridin' that lion a hundred feet at a jump, and quirtin' him down the flank with a rattlesnake.

It wasn't long before he saw a chuck-wagon, with a bunch of cow-boys squattin' around it. He rode up to that wagon, splittin' the air with his war-whoops, with that old lion a screechin', and that snake singin' his rattles.

When he came to the fire he grabbed the old cougar by the ear, jerked him back on his haunches, stepped off him, hung his snake around his neck, and looked the outfit over. Them cow-boys sat there sayin' less than nothin'.

Bill was hungry, and seein' a boilerful of beans cookin' on the fire, he scooped up a few handfuls and swallowed them, washin' them down with a few gallons of boilin' coffee out of the pot. Wipin' his mouth on a handful of prickly- pear cactus, Bill turned to the cow-boys and asked:

"Who's the boss around here?"

A big fellow about eight feet tall, with seven pistols and nine bowie knives in his belt, rose up, and, takin' off his hat, said:

"Stranger, I was; but you be."

Bill had many adventures with this outfit. It was about this time he staked out New Mexico, and used Arizona for a calf-pasture. It was here that he found his noted horse Widow Maker. He raised him from a colt on nitroglycerin and dynamite, and Bill was the only man that could throw a leg over him.

There wasn't anythin' that Bill couldn't ride, although I have heard of one occasion when he was thrown. He made a bet that he could ride an Oklahoma cyclone slick-heeled, without a saddle.

He met the cyclone, the worst that was ever known, up on the Kansas line. Bill eared that tornado down and climbed on its back. That cyclone did some pitchin' that is unbelievable, if it were not vouched for by many reliable witnesses. Down across Texas it went sunfishin', back-flippin', side-windin', knockin' down mountains, blowin' the holes out of the ground, and tyin' rivers into knots. The Staked Plains used to be heavily timbered until that big wind swiped the trees off and left it bare prairie.

Bill just sat up there, thumbin' that cyclone in the withers, floppin' it across the ears with his hat, and rollin'

a cigarette with one hand. He rode it through three States, but over in Arizona it got him.

When it saw it couldn't throw him, it rained out from under him. This is proved by the fact that it washed out the Grand Canyon. Bill came down in California. The spot where he lit is now known as Death Valley, a hole in the ground more than one hundred feet below sea-level, and the print of his hip-pockets can still be seen in the granite.

I have heard this story disputed in some of its details. Some historians claim that Bill wasn't thrown; that he slid down on a streak of lightin' without knockin' the ashes off his cigarette. It is also claimed that the Grand Canyon was dug by Bill one week when he went prospectin'; but the best authorities insist on the first version. They argue that the streak of lightnin' story comes from the habit he always had of usin' one to light his cigarette.

Bill was a great roper. In fact, he invented ropin'. Old-timers who admit they knew him say that his rope was as long as the equator, although the more conservative say that it was at least two feet shorter on one end. He used to rope a herd of cattle at one throw.

This skill once saved the life of a friend. The friend had tried to ride Widow-Maker one day, and was thrown so high he came down on top of Pike's Peak. He was in the middle of a

bad fix, because he couldn't get down, and seemed doomed to a lingerin' death on high.

Bill came to the rescue, and usin' only a short calf-loop, he roped his friend around the neck and jerked him down to safety in the valley, twenty thousand feet below. This man was always grateful, and became Bill's horse-wrangler at the time he staked out in New Mexico.

In his idle moments in New Mexico Bill amused himself puttin' thorns on the trees and horns on the toads. It was on this ranch he dug the Rio Grande and invented the centipede and the tarantula as a joke on his friends.

When the cow business was dull, Pecos Bill occasionally embarked in other ventures; for instance, at one time he took a contract to supply the S. P. Railroad with wood. He hired a few hundred Mexicans to chop and haul the wood to the railroad line. As pay for the job, Bill gave each Mexican one fourth of the wood he hauled.

These Mexicans are funny people. After they received their share of the wood they didn't know what to do with it; so Bill took it off their hands and never charged them a cent. On another occasion Bill took the job of buildin' the line fence that forms the boundary from El Paso across to the Pacific. He rounded up a herd of prairie-dogs and set them to dig holes, which by nature a prairie-dog likes to do.

Whenever one of them finished a nice hole and settled

down to live in it, Bill evicted him and stuck a fence-post in the hole. Everyone admired his foresight, except the prairie-dogs, and who cares what the prairie-dog thinks?

Old Bill was always a truthful man. To prove this, the cow-boys repeat one of his stories, which Bill claimed happened to him. Nobody ever disputed him; that is, no one who is alive now.

He threw in with a bunch of Kiowa Indians one time on a little huntin'-trip. It was about the time the buffalo were getting scarce, and Bill was huntin' with his famous squatter-hound named Norther.

Norther would run down a buffalo and hold him by the ear until Bill came up and skinned him alive. Then he would turn it loose to grow a new hide. The scheme worked all right in the summer, but in the winter most of them caught colds and died.

The stories of Bill's love affairs are especially numerous. One of them may be told. It is the sad tale of the fate of his bride, a winsome little maiden called Slue-Foot Sue. She was a famous rider herself, and Bill lost his heart when he saw her riding a catfish down the Rio Grande with only a surcingle. You must remember that the catfish in the Rio Grande are bigger than whales and twice as active.

Sue made a sad mistake, however, when she insisted on ridin' Widow-Maker on her weddin' day. The old horse

threw her so high she had to duck her head to let the moon go by. Unfortunately, she was wearin' her weddin'-gown, and in those days the women wore those big steel-spring bustles. Well, when Sue lit, she naturally bounced, and every time she came down she bounced again. It was an awful' sad sight to see Bill implorin' her to quit her bouncin' and not be so nervous; but Sue kept right on, up and down, weepin', and throwin' kisses to her distracted lover, and carryin' on as a bride would naturally do under those circumstances.

She bounced for three days and four nights, and Bill finally had to shoot her to keep her from starvin' to death. It was mighty tragic. Bill never got over it. Of course, he married lots of women after that. In fact, it was one of his weaknesses; but none of them filled the place in his heart once held by Slue-Foot Sue, his bouncin' bride. . . .

There is a great difference of opinon as to the manner of Bill's demise. Many claim that it was his drinkin' habits that killed him. You see, Bill got so that liquor didn't have any kick for him, and he fell into the habit of drinkin' strychnine and other forms of wolf pison.

Even the wolf bait lost its effect, and he got to putting' fish-hooks and barbed wire in his toddy. It was the barbed wire that finally killed him. It rusted his interior and gave him indigestion. He wasted to a mere skeleton, weighin' not more than two tons; then up and died, and went to his infernal reward.

Many of the border bards who knew Pecos Bill at his best have a different account of his death.

They say that he met a man from Boston one day, wearing a mail-order cow-boy outfit, and askin' fool questions about the West; and poor old Bill laid down and laughed himself to death.

John Henry
Robert Carola

Some children are born with silver spoons in their mouths—John Henry was born with a hammer in his hand.

According to legend, John Henry was an African American slave born in Alabama in the 1840's, and when he was still a little boy he proclaimed that he would become a steel-driver before he was twenty-one. And he did. But he also knew from his early days as a steel-driver that he would die with his hammer in his hand.

When the Civil War ended in 1865 the Chesapeake & Ohio Railroad Company opened new railroad lines through West Virginia that allowed for the westward move establish-

ment of new towns and sites for the timber and coal-mining industries.

The work was temporarily stalled when the tracks reached the Allegheny Mountains, where tunnels had to be built through the mountains by blasting with dynamite. The men who set the dynamite by pounding holes in the rock with hammer and drills were called steel-drivers, and the strongest driver was John Henry.

All the workers were African American. Many were believed to be convicts leased to the railroad company by penitentiaries, and most were ex-slaves, as John Henry was. (It is unlikely that John Henry was a convict because the only John Henry in prison at the time was only 5 feet, 1 ¼ inches tall—not the legendary John Henry's height and weight of over 6 feet and more than 200 pounds, a giant among the other workers.)

John Henry helped lay tracks like everyone else, but he gained fame striking a hand drill with his hammer against a chisel to break through the Allegheny Mountains that separated Kentucky, Tennessee, and West Virginia from Virginia and North and South Carolina. As he worked all day he sang how no hammer rang like his.

But it all changed one morning when John Henry and the other workers were blasting through a mountain to build the Great Bend, or Big Bend, Tunnel in west Virginia. The foreman announced that a new steam-powered drill would be

used to complete the tunnel. But John Henry swore he would die before he let a machine beat him and his crew. A competition was arranged.

John Henry switched to heavier than usual hammers and by the end of the day he had drilled fourteen feet to the machine's nine feet. The workers cheered, not noticing that John Henry was staggering.

John Henry had won the contest, but he had to pay with his life, collapsing among the shattered rock and powdery dust he had created. Before he died he asked for a drink of water, and said, "I beat the machine, but I'm dead, Lawd, I'm dead."

Legend says he was buried nearby, so that every locomotive that passed by could slow down to pay their respects to the one-and-only greatest steel-driving man who ever lived—and who had died fighting for the men who were not as strong as he, but still had to work for the boss. John Henry still represents all underdogs, not only blacks, and stands for the strength and courage of the working class of a whole country rebuilding itself after a terrible Civil War, and for the United States of America itself.

Coda: The Work Song
Railroad workers and other men who functioned as a coordinated group (such as a chain gang) sang work songs to act out

a rhythm and pace as they worked. Steel-driving crews would all lift the railroad track at the same time—the signal was a pronounced "huh" at the end of a line in the song that told the men to push their picks down to lift up the rail.

Example: This old hammer, *huh*
        Killed John Henry, *huh*
        Killed my brother, *huh*
        Won't kill me, *huh*
        Won't kill me, *huh*

Steel-driving placed dangerous physical strain on the men. Many men died under the strain. Part of the purpose of the song was to slow the work tempo to prolong the lives of the workers.

THE BALLAD OF JOHN HENRY
FOLKSONG

When John Henry was a little lad
A-holding of his papa's hand,
Says "If I live until I'm twenty-one.
I'm goin' to make a steel-driving man."

And Johnny said, when he was a man
He made his words come true,
He's the best steel-driver on the C&O Road,
He belongs to the steel-driving crew.

There are almost two hundred recorded versions of the Ballad of John Henry. The tale was passed along orally from the 1870s until folklorists discovered the song in 1909 when it was then written. This version was written down in 1915.

They brought John Henry from the white house
And took him to the tunnel to drive,
He drove so hard he broke his heart,
He laid down his hammer and he died.

I heard the walking boss coming,
Coming down the line;
I thought I heard the walking boss say,
"Johnny's in tunnel number nine."

John Henry standing on the right hand side,
The steam drill standing on the left,
He says "I'll beat that steam drill down,
Or I'll die with my hammer on my breast."

He placed the drill on the top of the rock,
The steam drill standing by his side,
He beat the steam drill an inch and a half
And he laid down his hammer and he died.

Before he died he said to his boss,
"Oh, bossman! How can it be,
"The rock is so hard and the steel is so rough,
I can feel my muscle giving way?"

Johnny said just before he died,
"I hope I'll meet you all above,
You take my hammer and wrap it in gold,
And give it to the girl I love."

When the people heard of poor Johnny's death
They could not stay at their home,
They all come out on the C&O line,
Where steel-driving Johnny used to roam.

If I die a railroad man
Go bury me under the tie,
So I can hear old number four
As she goes rolling by.

If you won't bury me under the ttrack,
Bury me under the sand,
With a pick and a shovel under my head
And a nine-pound hammer in my hand.

JOHNNY APPLESEED
ROBERT CAROLA

There really was a "Johnny Appleseed" whose real name was John Chapman. He was born in Massachusetts in 1774, and some say died while sleeping in a small apple orchard near Fort Wayne, Indiana in 1845 at the age of seventy-one. He was a pioneer nurseryman who provided apple-tree seedlings for early settlers in the Midwest. He collected unwanted apple seeds from Pennsylvania mills that processed apples to make cider. Then he dried the seeds and gave them to pioneers who were heading west. Soon "Johnny" was traveling westward himself, starting in about 1800 with new apple nurseries in the Alleghenies and into the midwest and beyond. Before long, apple orchards bloomed across the

country.

John Chapman was a colorful character who loved animals as well as people, knew his bible well and lived by its teachings, was an expert on medicinal herbs, and created friendships with the Indians who were grateful for his help in healing their sick and swore they heard him talking with animals he encountered. He had a dress code that couldn't be missed: He wore his long hair under a cooking pan, walked barefooted, wore torn pants and a "cape" made of an old coffee sack with holes cut out for his head and arms.

His eccentric behavior undoubtedly contributed to his death from exposure, but not before he had owned about 12,000 acres of farm and orchard, and had literally planted the seeds for the growth of the legend of "Johnny Appleseed." In 1871 W. D. Haley wrote an article in *Harper's New Monthly Magazine* about an eccentric pioneer named John Chapman, and soon stories, poems, plays, and books about Johnny Appleseed turned amazing truth into legendary American folklore.

When Chapman died in 1845, General Sam Houston addressed Congress in a tribute, saying "Farewell, dear old eccentric heart. Your labor has been a labor of love, and generations yet unborn will rise up and call you blessed." And so we do, and will.

JOHNNY APPLESEED:
A PIONEER HERO
R. D. HALEY

Among the heroes of endurance that was voluntary, and of action that was creative and sanguinary, there was one man whose name, seldom mentioned now save by some of the few surviving pioneers, deserves to be perpetuated.

The first reliable trace of our modest hero finds him in the territory of Ohio, in 1801, with a horse-load of apple seeds, which he planted in various places on and about the borders of Licking Creek, the first orchard thus originated by him being on the farm of Isaac Stadden, in what is now Licking County in the State of Ohio.

. . . Having planted his stock of seeds, he would

return to Pennsylvania for a fresh supply, and, as sacks made of any less substantial fabric would not endure the hard usage of the long trip through forests dense with underbrush and briers, he provided himself with leathern bags. Securely packed, the seeds were conveyed, sometimes on the back of a horse, and not infrequently on his own shoulders, either over a part of the old Indian trail that lead from Fort Duquesne to Detroit, by way of Fort Sandusky. . . which would require him to traverse a distance of one hundred and sixty-six miles in a west-northwest direction from Fort Duquesne in order to reach the Black Fork of the Mohican.

This region, although it is now densely populated, still possesses a romantic beauty that railroads and bustling towns can not obliterate—a country of forest-clad hills and green valleys, through which numerous bright streams flow on their way to the Ohio; but when Johnny Appleseed reached some lonely log-cabin he would find himself in veritable wilderness. . . . Johnny would shoulder his bag of apple seeds and with bare feet, penetrate to some remote spot that combined picturesqueness and fertility of soil, and there he would plant his seeds, place a slight inclosure around the place, and leave them to grow until the trees were large enough to be transplanted by the settlers, who, in the mean time, would have made their clearings in the vicinity. The sites chosen by him

are, many of them, well known, and are such as an artist or a poet would select—open places on the loamy lands that border the creeks—rich, secluded spots, hemmed in by giant trees, picturesque now, but fifty years ago, with their wild surroundings and the primal silence, they must have been tenfold more so.

. . . It was his custom, when he had been welcomed to some hospitable log-house after a weary day of journeying, to lie down on the puncheon floor, and, after inquiring if his auditors would hear "some news right fresh from heaven," produce his few tattered books, among which would be a New Testament, and read and expound until his uncultivated hearers would catch the spirit and glow of his enthusiasm, while they scarcely comprehended his language. A lady who knew him in his later years writes in the following terms of one of these domiciliary readings of poor, self-sacrificing Johnny Appleseed: "We can hear him read now, just as he did that summer day, when we were busy quilting up stairs, and he lay near the door, his vice rising denunciatory and thrilling—strong and loud as the roar of wind and waves, then soft and soothing as the balmy airs that quivered the morning glory leaves abut his gray beard. His was a strange eloquence at times, and he was undoubtedly a man of genius." What a scene is presented to our imagination! The interior of a primi

tive cabin, the wide, open fire-place, where a few sticks are burning beneath the iron pot, in which the evening meal is cooking; around the fire-place the attentive group, composed of the sturdy pioneer and his wife and children, listening with a reverential awe to the "news right fresh from heaven"; and reclining on the floor, clad in rags, but with his gray hairs glorified by the beams of the setting sun that flood through the open door and the unchinked logs of the humble building, this poor wanderer, with the gift of genus and eloquence, who believes with the faith of apostles and martyrs that God appointed him a mission in the wilderness to preach the Gospel of love, and plant apple seeds that shall produce orchards for the benefit of men and women and little children whom he has never seen. If there is a sublimer faith or a more genuine eloquence in richly decorated cathedrals and under brocade vestments, it would be worth a long journey to find it.

Next to his advocacy of his peculiar religious ideas, his enthusiasm for the cultivation of apple-trees in what he termed "the only proper way"—that is, from seed—was the absorbing object of his life. Upon this, as upon religion, he was eloquent in his appeals. He would describe the growing and ripening fruit as such a rare and beautiful gift of the Almighty with words that became pictures, until his hearers could almost see its manifold forms of beauty present before them.

To his eloquence on this subject, as well as to his actual labors in planting nurseries, the country over which he traveled for so many years is largely indebted for its numerous orchards. But he denounced as absolute wickedness all devices of pruning and grafting, and would speak of the act of cutting a tree as if it were a cruelty inflicted upon a sentient being.

THE OLD CHISHOLM TRAIL
FOLKSONG

Come along boys, and listen to my tale
I'll tell you of my troubles on the old Chisholm
trail.

[Refrain:]
Come a ti yi yippee, come a ti yi yea,
Come a ti yi yippee, come a ti yi yea.

Oh, a ten-dollar hoss and a forty-dollar saddle,
And I'm goin' to punchin' Texas cattle.

[Refrain]

I wake in the mornin' afore daylight,
And afore I sleep the moon shines bright.

[Refrain]
It's cloudy in the west, a-lookin' like rain,
And my durned old slicker's in the wagon again.

[Refrain]
No chaps, no slicker, and it's pourin' down rain,
And I swear, by gosh, I'll never night-herd again.

[Refrain]
Feet in the stirrups and seat in the saddle,
I hung and rattled with them long-horn cattle.

[Refrain]
The wind commenced to blow, and the rain
        began to fall,
Hit looked, by grab, like we was goin' to lose
        'em all.

[Refrain]
I don't give a darn if they never do stop;
I'll ride as long as an eight-day clock.

[Refrain]
We rounded 'em up and put 'em on the cars,
And that was the last of the old Two Bars.

[Refrain]
Oh, it's bacon and beans most every day,
I'd as soon be a-eatin' prairie hay.

[Refrain]
I went to the boss to draw my roll,
He had it figgered out I was nine dollars in the
         hole.

[Refrain]
Goin' back to town to draw my money,
Goin' back home to see my honey.

[Refrain]
With my knees in the saddle and my seat in the
         sky,
I'll quit punchin' cows in the sweet by and by.

[Refrain]

THE COWBOY'S LAMENT
FOLKSONG

As I walked out in the streets of Laredo,
As I walked out in Laredo one day,
I spied a poor cowboy wrapped up in white
        linen,
Wrapped up in white linen as cold as the clay.

"Oh, beat the drum slowly and play the fife
        lowly,
Play the dead march as you carry me along;
Take me to the green valley, there lay the sod
        o'er me,
For I'm a young cowboy and I know I've done
        wrong.

"I see by your outfit that you are a cowboy" --
These words he did say as I boldly stepped by.
"Come sit down beside me and hear my sad
       story;
I am shot in the breast and I know I must die.

"Let sixteen gamblers come handle my coffin
Let sixteen cowboys come sing me a song.
Take me to the graveyard and lay the sod o'er
       me,
For I'm a poor cowboy and I know I've done
       wrong.

"My friends and relations they live in the
       Nation,
They know not where their boy has gone.
He first came to Texas and hired to a ranch
       man,
Oh, I'm a young cowboy and I know I've done
       wrong.

"It was once in the saddle I used to go dashing,
It was once in the saddle I used to go gay;
First to the dram-house and then to the card-

house;
Got shot in the breast and I am dying today.

"Get six jolly cowboyus to carry my coffin;
Get six pretty maidens to bear up my pall.
Put bunches of roses all over my coffin,
Put roses to deaden the sods as they fall.

"Then swing your rope slowly and rattle your
      spurs lowly,
And give a wild whoop as you carry me along,
And in the grave throw me and roll the sod o'er
      me,
For I'm a young cowboy and I know I've done
wrong.

"Oh, bury beside me my knife and six-shooter,
My spurs on my heel, my rifle by my side,
And over my coffin put a bottle of brandy,
That the cowboys may drink as they carry me
      along.

"Go bring me a cup, a cup of cold water,
To cool my parched lips," the cowboy then said;
Before I returned his soul had departed,

And gone to the round-up -- the cowboy was
    dead.

We beat the drum slowly and played the fife
    lowly,
And bitterly wept as we bore him along;
For we all loved our comrade, so brave, young
    and handsome,
We all loved our comrade although he'd done
    wrong.

GIT ALONG, LITTLE DOGIES
FOLKSONG

As I was a-walking one morning for
	pleasure,
I spied a young cowpuncher a-riding alone.
His hat was throwed back and his spurs was a-
	jinglin',
As he approached me a-singin' this song.

Whoopee ti yi yo, git along, little dogies,
It's your misfortune and none of my own,
Whoopee ti yi yo, git along, little dogies,
For you know Wyoming will be your new home.

Some fellows goes up the trail for pleasure,
But that's where they've got it most awfully
         wrong,
For you haven't an idea the trouble they give
         us,
As we go a-drivin' them dogies along.

Whoopee ti yi yo, git along, little dogies,
It's your misfortune and none of my own,
Whoopee ti yi yo, git along, little dogies,
For you know Wyoming will be your new home.

A Gift from St. Nicholas

Charles M. Skinner

Among the people leaving old Amsterdam for a home in New Amsterdam before the latter town was much more than come to its majority was Claas Schlaschenschlinger, who practiced the profession of cobbler in a little house at the head of New Street and had money enough to entitle him to wear eight pairs of breeches at once, and therefore to cut a wide figure in the society of the new metropolis. He had a pond behind his house, where he kept geese that multiplied to his profit, and he was calmly content with his lot—in fact, with his house and lot—till he fell in love. Nobody is calm or contented after that happens to him. His love would have been a successful enterprise had not the

coquettish Anitje, on whom his heart was set, been desired by the burgomaster, Roeloffsen. There were other young women in the colony who might have endured that person's temper, his homeliness, his stinginess, for the sake of the comfortable widowhood promised by his advancing years, because he was the richest man in town; but Anitje was none of such. She was too good of an American already to sell herself for money or position, so she accepted Claas, to the infinite joy of that aspiring artisan. Among his other mean qualities Roeloffsen now developed a revengeful disposition, for, by the time Claas and Anitje were comfortably, and, as they fancied, securely settled, and were occupied in the rearing of an annually increasing family, the burgomaster began a series of expensive and disconcerting improvements,—extending streets through pastures, filling hollows, lowering mounds, bridging rills, and draining puddles. Claas's pond had to go. The money for his geese tidied him over until the next improvement, but the assessment for cutting trees and guttering the street and laying a walk past Claas's house to a marsh, took all the silver he had stored in the old pewter teapot. Worst of all, there arrived from Holland, about this time, to complete his ruin, a blacksmith who filled the soles and heels of New Amsterdam with hobnails, which enabled the wearer to preserve a pair of boots for years, and announced their comings and goings on the plank walks and brick pavements and tavern floors with a

clatter like a revolution. So it fell out on Christmas eve of a certain year that Claas, his wife, his six children, and his cat sat before a meager fire and heard the wind howl and the snow dash against the panes. They digested their supper of bread and cheese and beer with deplorable facility, and bleakly wondered what there would be for breakfast.

Claas sighed forth his sorrow that he had ever left Holland. What could he do to carry him through another week? He might sell the silver clasps on the bible. Fie! It had been his mother's, and beside—to deface the Good Book! Well, then, what? He sprang up with a laugh, for it had just come to him that on the morning of his departure for America he had found in his best stockings a meerschaum pipe, so beautifully dyed by some faithful smoker that no mere cobbler was fit to use it. Without a question it had been a gift from St. Nicholas, his name-saint. A pipe of such a rich mahogany color was worth the price of a Christmas dinner, and pork and tea for several days beside. He went to the old chest and unburied it from a quantity of gear that had come from the old country with him, and took it to the window, and rubbed it carefully on his sleeve. A gust of wind filled the room. Claas cried, "Now, which of you children will do such a thing as not to keep the house shut in weathers like these?" and started to close the door, when he bumped into a little portly stranger who had entered and stood regarding Claas with twinkling eyes.

"Eh? Did somebody call me?" asked the unknown. "Well, seeing that I am in, and have been out there in the cold for hours, I will make free to warm myself at your fire."

The family having made room for him before the excuse for a blaze, the visitor rubbed his glowing cheeks and shining nose and spread his fingers over the ashes. "I must say, Mynheer Schlaschenschlinger," said he, "that you are not very hospitable. You might at least put another couple of logs on the hearth. Humph! 'In need, one learns to know one's friends.' "

"There are more Faderland proverbs than that, also, and one is, 'It is hard combing when there is no hair.' "

"Pooh, pooh! Never talk to me of that. Let me remind you of another: 'Who gives from what he has deserves to live.' "

"Ah, mynheer," answered Claas, with a rueful countenance, "no man has ever been turned from my hearth; but I have nothing left to burn, unless it is my house."

"Aha! Is it so? Been wasting your substance, I see. Well, then, 'Who burns himself must sit on the blisters.' There, never mind; I was jesting. 'A good understanding needs only half a word.' " And before Claas could prevent it the stranger had cracked a fine rosewood cane over his knee and tossed it on the embers. Instantly it blazed up merrily, giving as much heat as an armful of hickory logs, so that the cat roused in astonishment at the singeing of her tail and was fain to crawl

to a cool corner; and the cane burned for ever so long without going out, making the place seem cheery and home-like once more. Presently the guest began to rub his paunch and look wistfully at the cupboard, glancing aside at the cobbler and his wife, as if wondering how long they would be in taking a hint. Finally he blurted, "I've had no dinner, and I hoped I might be asked to share a bite and sup. This, you know, is Christmas eve."

Claas winced. "You should be welcome with gladness, if we had some things to eat that we could offer to you."

"Never tell me that you've had your supper. I can eat anything. 'Hunger makes raw beans sweet.'"

"It is hard, what I have to tell. It is that we have no beans."

"Look here, Claas, I don't think you intend to be mean. Never trouble about the beans. A cut from that fowl will do, for it is a fowl I see on that shelf, isn't it? And there is no mistaking that big bread-loaf. And are my eyes done dim with the heat, or are those cookies and olykoeks and mince pies? And never tell me it is water you keep in that bottle."

Claas eyed his friend wearily, yet warily, for he doubted but the little man was daft, while Anitje went to the cupboard to show the visitor how well he was mistaken; that his eyes had turned the flickering shadows and reflections into things that were not there; but she threw up her hands and cried

aloud; then ran to Claas with a roast goose on a platter, whereon Claas cried louder, and the offspring cried loudest.

" 'Better a half egg than an empty shell,' as we say in Amsterdam," remarked the ruddy man with a sarcastic wink, and his finger at his nose.

Candles were lighted, and in a minute a brave array of good things smoked on the table, for the wonder of it was that except the wine and schnapps, which were cold and fragrant, they seemed to have come but then from the oven.

"Now, then," said the stranger, beaming, " 'one may not give away his shirt if not sure of his skirt,' as we used to say in Holland, but I think you can spare me a plate of that goose."

So they fell to and feasted themselves in the merriest humor, and the shavers flocked to the knee of the man with the twinkling eyes, who was full of quips and stories, and they pledged one another in glasses of Rhenish—Claas dimly wondering where he had bought those handsome glasses—and in the end the stranger gave Vrou Anitje a tremendous smack, which only made her blush and Claas to grin, for those greetings were duties and compliments in the simple days. Then Claas showed the pipe he had intended to sell, whereon the stranger cried, "That pipe! I know it. John Calvin used to smoke it. It is a lucky pipe. You must keep it all your days and leave it to your children. Whoop! What's all that? " For at this

moment the boys of the neighborhood, who were allowed on this one night to sit up later than nine o'clock, or had been called by their indulgent parents, greeted their holiday by firing their little cannon.

"Midnight!" exclaimed the twinkling little man. "I must be off. Merry Christmas and Happy New Year to you all. Good night."

And with that the stranger arose and bowed himself into the chimney. Now, whether he stamped among the ashes and sent up such a cloud as to blind them all,—for it is certain their eyes were watery and they fell a-sneezing, —or whether the little gentleman was so very lively that he got away through the door before they could say "Jack Robinson,"— which they never did say, there being no such man in the colony—Claas and his wife and children could never agree, Anitje and the girls insisting that he went up the chimney, as if he had been blown away in the draft. In the morning, when the wife swept the hearth before starting a new fire, she heard the chink of silver, and there in the ashes she found a fat purse bearing the words, "A Gift from St. Nicholas."

While she and her husband were marveling properly upon this an increasing gabble of voices was heard outside, and behold, there was half the town populace staring up at their windows and expressing great astonishment. And with reason, for the house was no longer of wood, but of brick.

There was talk of arresting Claas and his family as wizards and dangerous to the well-being of the State, but he told so straight a story, and showed such substantial evidences of his new prosperity, that they made him an alderman instead. "The Dutch House," as they called it, was for many years a landmark. When it was torn down, by an alien of British origin, the workmen were slapped about the sconce by unseen hands and had laths and slats vehemently applied to their sitting parts so that the neighbors said St. Nicholas was protecting his own.

A Visit from St. Nicholas
Clement C. Moore

'Twas the night before Christmas, when all
    through the house,
Not a creature was stirring, not even a mouse;
The stockings were all hung by the chimney
    with care,
In hopes that St. Nicholas soon would be there;
The children were nestled all snug in their beds,
While visions of sugar-plums danced in their
    heads;
And Mamma in her 'kerchief, and I in my cap,
Had just settled down for a long winter's nap;—
When out on the lawn there arose such a clatter,
I sprang from my bed to see what was the
    matter.
Away to the window I flew like a flash,

Tore open the shutters and threw up the sash.
The moon on the breast of the new-fallen
　　　snow,
Gave the luster of mid-day to objects below,
When, what to my wondering eyes should
　　　appear,
But a miniature sleigh, and eight tiny reindeer,
With a little old driver, so lively and quick,
I knew in a moment it must be St. Nick.
More rapid than eagles his coursers they came,
And he whistled and shouted, and called them
　　　by name:
"Now, *Dasher!* now, *Dancer!* now, *Prancer* and
　　　Vixen!
On *Comet!* on, *Cupid!* on, *Donder* and *Blitzen!*
To the top of the porch! To the top of the wall!
Now dash away! dash away! dash away all!
As dry leaves that before the wild hurricane fly,
When they meet with an obstacle, mount to the
　　　sky;
So up to the house-top the coursers they flew

With the sleigh full of Toys, and St. Nicholas
　　　too.
And then, in a twinkling, I heard on the roof

The prancing and pawing of each little hoof—
As I drew in my head, and was turning around,
Down the chimney St. Nicholas came with a
     bound.
He was dressed all in furs from his head to his
     foot,
And his clothes were all tarnished with ashes
     and soot;
A bundle of Toys he had flung on his back,
And he looked like a peddler just opening his
     pack.
His eyes—how they twinkled! His dimples how
     merry!
His cheeks were like roses, his nose like a
     cherry!
His droll little mouth was drawn up like bow,
And the beard on his chin was as white as the
     snow;
The stump of a pipe he held tight in his teeth,
And the smoke it encircled his head like a
     wreath;
He was chubby and plump, a right jolly old elf;
And I laughed when I saw him, in spite of
     myself;
A wink of his eye and a twist of his head

Soon gave me to know I had nothing to dread;
He spoke not a word, but went straight to his
work,
And filled all the stockings; then turned with a
jerk,
And laying his finger aside of his nose,
And giving a nod, up the chimney he rose,
He sprang to his sleigh, to his team gave a
whistle,
And away they all flew like the down of a thistle.
But I heard him exclaim, ere he drove out of
sight,
"Happy Christmas to all, and to all a good
night!"